THE SEVEN SEAT

A True Story of Rowing, Revenge, and Redemption

DANIEL J. BOYNE

Guilford, Connecticut

An imprint of The Rowman & Littlefield Publishing Group, Inc.
4501 Forbes Blvd., Ste. 200
Lanham, MD 20706
www.rowman.com

Distributed by NATIONAL BOOK NETWORK

British Library Cataloguing in Publication Information available

Library of Congress Cataloging-in-Publication Data available

ISBN 978-1-4930-4354-5 (hardcover)
ISBN 978-1-4930-4355-2 (e-book)

♾™ The paper used in this publication meets the minimum requirements of American National Standard for Information Sciences—Permanence of Paper for Printed Library Materials, ANSI/NISO Z39.48-1992.

"We cared for nothing except for amusing ourselves and rowing, for we all worshiped the oar . . ."

—GUY DE MAUPASSANT, MOUCHE

TABLE OF CONTENTS

FOREWORD

The first year at university can be one of the most exhilarating and fulfilling yet equally confusing and even jarring experiences of a young adult life; the cacophony of new and diverse personalities combined with a sudden blitz of freedom, unforeseen obligations, and open-ended opportunities unlike anything you've ever experienced before. Add to that your first year on a rowing team, and it soon becomes one of the most intense experiences imaginable.

For many students, joining and becoming part of an athletic team is not only a daunting challenge, but also a deeply organizing influence that can give context to the onslaught of new impressions and responsibilities.

For experienced rowers and walk-on athletes alike (perhaps more so for walk-on athletes, a dying breed in our current times), the memories from that first year endure in an almost tactile way; the first ride to the boathouse, the first pass through the locker room, the first row, and the proximity of a strange new body of water beneath you, just inches away—all remain vivid for decades.

In my own first year of rowing, before frosh were absorbed into varsity programs, a freshman rowing squad was still a team unto itself, with its own coach, race times, practice times, rituals, and culture—and certainly its own personality. Many of us from that team recall each other as we were back then, and still refer to one another by nicknames bestowed in the first weeks and days of fall freshman rowing—names such as Tunes, Birdman, KFS, Breaks, Shakes, V, the Rowin' Samoan, Fust, Pas de Couilles, Rasta, Sleaze, Call Me Mike, Handkerchief Head, Pops (our coach), and more.

And whether it was a good year or a bad year for your team, there was a narrative throughput that was stronger and more vivid than almost any other of a rowing career. The massive mash-up of regional dialects, attitudes, and experiences is a lot to absorb, and many of the first impressions you have of one another stick forever.

Daniel Boyne captures that full tableau for himself and his Trinity cohorts here in *The Seven Seat*, parts of which we worked on together and serialized on row2k. With each new chapter, delivered to me almost at the moment it had been written, readers were able to follow along with the unexpected revelations of the layers of personality and depth of Boyne's teammates during moments away from the river, the role the coaches began to play in their college life, extracurricular activities that the coach and other authority figures were better off not knowing about, a few dicey moments shoulder-deep in a cold river, of course some matters of the heart, and a lot of pretty serious rowing.

In this "creative nonfiction" (as Boyne describes it) narrative of his first year at Trinity, we encounter multifaceted characters, comedians, rivals, leaders, fools, and more; Boyne's portrayal of his own fierce and loyal frosh coach is rich and illustrative, as are his portrayals of his teammates. Boyne's female characters are dimensional as well, which is not a surprise from the author of *Red Rose Crew*, the story of the 1975 U.S. women's eight.

The experiences away from the water that Boyne recounts are no less vivid nor essential, including the illicit climbing of storied architecture, various frat house hijinks, and more. Along the way Boyne simultaneously enhances and unmasks the reputations of rowing legends, and wins a few races. Throughout it all Boyne is a somewhat-serious and self-aware observer (arguably as befits a seven seat), which does not prevent him from appreciating and engaging with the somewhat less-studied sides of the other characters in the story.

It is also a revenge story, and any high school rower whose high school team was split into different factions at different universities knows both how intense and important those instant rivalries with former teammates can be. Certainly many remember the first time they looked across at the starting line and saw their former boat mates in the same seat but in the neighboring boat; *The Seven Seat* derives much of its narrative drive from just that moment.

Many rowers have a similar book stuck in their head, and Boyne offers a way for readers to recall those experiences, even if they are not inclined to write them down. As with many memoirs, a powerful part of the experience of reading along with Boyne is how the memories of our own first escapades in the sport and as college students and budding adults are unearthed and reignited.

Boyne's story is honest as well. He and his teammates and coaches are likable but certainly not perfect, and as I read I was reminded more than once of William Finnegan's unflinching memoir *Barbarian Days: A Surfing Life*—which of course won the Pulitzer Prize for Biography in 2016. It is unlikely that a book about rowing in Connecticut and Philadelphia will reach those heights, but there are similarities nonetheless.

As Boyne notes in the serialized version on row2k, the book is a "work of 'creative nonfiction,'" which means that it is more or less true." With some names changed, it does become something of a roman à clef, although it was vivid enough for many of the renamed folks such that, as we posted each chapter, I received emails along the lines of "Uh-oh, I may show up in the next chapter, and probably as a villain." I won't reveal if any of these folks made it into the book, but certainly many of us will find a little bit of ourselves and our old teammates in the college paths, rooftops, boathouses, and rowing seats in these pages.

—Ed Hewitt

INTRODUCTION

Rowing, one of the oldest athletic endeavors in the Western world, has finally captured the attention of the mainstream public, after hiding in plain sight for many decades. Films and books have begun to proliferate, providing a broader palette to the many colors and shades of the sport and adding texture to the strange tribe of modern-day Vikings who move across water with an oar in their hands. But when I was entering the sport, back in the 1970s, there were only a few books on rowing, and most of them were training manuals, tedious and dry.

Then, in 1985, the celebrated journalist David Halberstam wrote *The Amateurs* and captured the raw beauty of rowing. Short, terse, and devoid of purple prose, the little book rang true in the rowing world and opened the door to other literary efforts.

I'd recently graduated from Trinity College in Hartford, Connecticut, and when *The Amateurs* came out I took a silent vow that I would try to write a narrative, equal in measure. I was fortunate enough to fulfill my ambitions with three offerings—*The Red Rose Crew, Kelly,* and *Essential Sculling.* I thought I was done. Yet in the back of my mind, a personal narrative of my college rowing days was still brewing—a lighthearted tale with a twist of revenge. *The Seven Seat* is that story. In a way it is a whimsical little tale, not too ambitious in scope, but rather a freshman-year frolic that is primarily meant to amuse. On the other hand, scattered throughout these pages are some unique glimpses into the rowing world that may offer deeper insights.

Many rowing narratives, like the sport itself, are overly serious in nature. In those fine books, men and women win Olympic gold medals, row across the Atlantic, survive divorce, or win World Wars. I wrote *The Seven Seat*, in part, to break out of this heroic mode, and make readers laugh as they learn about the life of an ordinary bunch of college oarsmen in the 1970s—a group of scrawny, nonrecruited lightweights. What we accomplished with our oars might still be seen as inspirational, but what we did off the water was equally entertaining. After all, heroism can get tedious when it lacks the balance of everyday life and all of its humorous absurdities.

Having been in the rowing world now for fourscore years—first as an amateur competitor, then a coach, a writer, and even a film consultant for *The Social Network*—my focus has always been firmly rooted in celebrating the underdog, but it has shifted more and more toward those who are just "ordinary folk." Rowing in general has followed this trend and finally opened its arms to the general public. This is not only refreshing but more in keeping with its original roots, and in my opinion the sport should be celebrated for its own sake and not just for those who reach the top pinnacles.

Conversely, on the collegiate level, a lot has changed since the days when this story took place. Trinity College no longer has lightweight crew, an unfortunate loss for my alma mater, and the recruiting of high school athletes has now become a serious business, with big athletic incentives and better coaching salaries in play. At the elite level, professionalism has slowly crept back into the sport, with prize races offered at the Head of the Charles and elsewhere, as they once were in the late nineteenth century. But back in the days of disco, where this story begins, we were all still very much amateurs, with no idea what we were getting ourselves into, and it is in that spirit of innocence that *The Seven Seat* unfolds and hopefully succeeds in rendering the simple joys of freshman crew.

(Author's Note: This is a work of "creative nonfiction," which means that it is more or less true. Some of the characters' names have been altered, mostly to protect them from any factual errors on my part.)

CHAPTER ONE

The Walk On

What is it about those first fall days in New England that infuses us with the vigor to change our lives? Is it simply the end of summer's languid embrace, exchanged for the sobering chill of September? Is it the fading, golden light at the beginning and end of each day, producing a sense of urgency? As a freshman entering Trinity College in Hartford, Connecticut, I thought little about these philosophical musings and felt only the raw excitement in the air.

Something primitive was stirring, and it quickened my steps as I moved my trunk of belongings into the old brick dorms of Jarvis Hall.

Set high on the western slope of the city, Trinity was the second-oldest school in the state, built partly to provide an alternative to Yale, the existing Ivy League offering. Jarvis was one of the four original dorms on campus that configured the main quad, and although its rooms had recently been downsized to accommodate more students, its outer façade, at least, made it picture-worthy for my baggage-hauling parents. My mother took a quick sniff of the room and gave it her seal of approval; my father handed me a twenty-dollar bill and said: "Spend it wisely." Then I was left to my own devices.

I was paired with a basketball player named Jim Minahan, whose rangy, muscular stature dwarfed my emaciated runner's build, but we immediately hit it off. Despite our physical differences, "Slim Jim" and I were both public school kids, unused to navigating the social terrain of an elite private institution. We decided to stick together. On the way to our first meal, we strolled down the one-hundred-year-old promenade known as "The Long Walk" and got our first glimpse of girls donning Fair Isle sweaters and perfectly coiffed shoulder-length hair, and guys in Nantucket red shorts wielding lacrosse sticks like shillelaghs.

We tried not to gawk like a couple of tourists, but the high Victorian Gothic architecture of Seabury Hall, Northam Towers, and Jarvis Hall was a tad intimidating to us, clad in our Levi's and T-shirts. By contrast, the prep school kids breezed along the main quad as if it was an all-too-familiar stage, wearing their privilege and brightly colored clothing like exotic plumage.

The college dining hall, thankfully, was a great class leveler, and there was nothing about either the eating arrangements or the meal itself that could make anyone feel entitled. We shuffled through the cafeteria line and ate the same mass-produced food as the preppies. Breaking bread brought everyone into a temporary communion. After dinner I unwisely picked the top bunk, and Jim quickly discovered the juvenile pleasure of pressing his long legs up against my mattress and bouncing me up and down before bedtime. I responded in turn by dropping some unsavory food items I'd secreted from the dining hall down onto his oversize head. In short, we got along just fine.

Naturally I was going to have to do some sport, however, or our budding friendship would suffer.

Why did I decide on rowing? I'd noticed the crew people, gathered together at a special table in the dining hall set up to recruit newbies like me, but I'd always been kind of a loner, not inclined to join things. Still, there was a sense of genuine oddity about these oarsmen that made me curious, for they were a motley-looking group of athletes—heavyweights and lightweights, men and women—all standing together proudly, like a circus troupe. They'd strategically positioned their recruiting table at the dining hall entryway, like a gate, so that you couldn't pass by without taking note of them.

"What are you looking at, Fresh Meat?" said a girl with a deep voice and a slight Southern drawl. "Haven't you ever seen a girl with muscles before?"

She flexed her biceps at me and smiled, then introduced herself as the women's captain, Cynda Davis.

One of the heavyweight men suddenly barked at me as I tried to pass by, a giant nicknamed Mongo.

"Ah, a lightweight," he said. "I eat lightweights!"

Davis laughed at the crude remark, which had no doubt been uttered many times before. Thankfully Mongo was not inclined toward cannibalism, although he had in fact bitten off the edge of a wooden bar at a local pub named the *Nutshell*. Other weird stories, too, soon emerged about the crew people. My overall impression was that the Trinity rowers were a different breed of athlete, composed largely of castaways and rejects from other sports, ex-runners and -swimmers, and even a few ballplayers whose knees had suffered repeated abuse from quick, lateral movements. Yet they had an undeniable, collective pride and a devil-may-care attitude toward noncrew folk. I also learned that rowing, unlike other sports like lacrosse or soccer, could be learned within a season or two.

I'd actually tried out single sculling the past summer at a place called Blood Street Sculls, in Old Lyme, Connecticut, a town better known for infectious deer ticks than rowing. My introduction to the sport, however, had proven to be quite challenging, so I'd kept that experience under my hat. I certainly enjoyed being out on the water, for I'd grown up around boats and the ocean, but the technical challenges of oarsmanship initially eluded me. Admittedly I was more of a sailor than a rower, preferring to use the twin resources of the wind and my own wits for propulsion, rather than the blind brute force that rowing seemed to require.

My old British coach at Blood Street, Ernest Arlett, was less than thrilled with my progress on Roger's Lake, for he had high standards that I repeatedly failed to meet. I capsized with great frequency and managed to exhibit nearly all of the technical flaws that one could possibly muster—lifting my shoulders too early in the drive, digging the blades too deep, and banging my hands together through the middle of the stroke until they made a bloody mess all over the oar handles. The name "Blood Street Sculls" took on an entirely different meaning for me that summer, and the only mark I managed to leave on their program was my DNA.

Still, I liked the *idea* of rowing, or rather the way it looked when it was done well, and that summer I'd at least persisted to a level that was not too embarrassing. So, after repeatedly seeing the crew posters that peppered every bulletin board on campus, I decided to at least show up for the preliminary meeting and check it out—after all, my sister was rowing at Mount Holyoke for her second year and loving it. Team rowing, she assured me, was much different from single sculling, and all crew coaches weren't so irascible and hard to please as my first one at Blood Street.

As it turned out, Charlie Poole, the freshman coach, was indeed the polar opposite of Coach Arlett—young, gregarious, and built like a Greek deity. Not only was he a recent Trinity grad, but also the stroke of an exceptional crew that had won the prestigious Henley Royal Regatta in 1976. During the recruiting pitch, we all sat around in the field house and watched a film called *Symphony of Motion*, which displayed the rigors and Zen-like beauty of the sport, and then an ABC *Wide World of Sports* clip that showed Poole stroking his varsity heavyweight crew brilliantly down the straight, two-lane course at Henley. Toward the end of the race, the British announcer calmly observed, "Trinity is well ahead now, and the stroke is lengthening out his strokes in the final stretch." The implication, I later learned, was that it was bad form to trounce another crew, and Poole was allowing the losers to save face.

This was an entirely new concept for me in athletics, and in life in general, for I'd been taught by my high school coaches to try and dominate the other team and leave them completely devastated. The gentlemanly attitude, however, matched Poole's overall demeanor, for he was an enthusiastic but self-effacing advocate for his sport. Physically he looked like no other athlete I'd ever seen, with a chiseled physique and a broad, toothy smile that could have landed him on the front cover of any bodybuilding magazine. Yet his stature wasn't manufactured, or oddly muscle bound—it seemed as natural and plain as the plaid lumberjack shirt he wore and the broad, inviting smile on his face.

If crew produced people like this, I wanted in.

Coach Poole looked me over, suppressed a frown, and then asked me how much I weighed. I'd been running cross-country all through high school, and I was a scrawny-looking beanpole.

"About 137," I said, adding a few pounds for good measure.

Poole scratched his head and said, "Well, we could certainly use another coxswain on the team . . ."

My spirits immediately sank, as that was definitely not what I had in mind—I wanted to be an oarsman. I quickly mentioned that I'd sculled before, and Poole asked me for some details. In a quiet but determined voice, I told him that I'd advanced into a racing shell the past summer at Blood Street under the tutelage of Ernie Arlett. Naturally I didn't mention that my outings on Roger's Lake were riddled with bad strokes and frequent dunkings.

His expression immediately changed.

"Well, in that case, let's see how you do with one oar!" he said, beaming.

I smiled back, for I'd narrowly escaped the fate of being culled from the herd and made into a coxswain.

"By the way," he said, "we have an old wooden single at the boathouse that you can always take out if there are too many people for practice. I'd love to see how you handle it!"

The smile slowly faded from my lips.

But fall was in the air, and with it came the promise of new possibility.

CHAPTER TWO

Beatings Make You Stronger

Before we go any further with this quasi-heroic rowing tale, I should probably confess that back in grade school I had a knack for getting beaten up. I only mention this embarrassing biographical detail to launch an unschooled theory about the dark psychological roots of rowing, not often discussed: namely, physical abuse and the ability to endure pain can often be quite useful.

Now whether or not these two qualities are necessary for rowing is debatable. Peter Haining, a former Scottish lightweight sculler, once admitted to me matter-of-factly that his father used to take him out on Loch Lomond in a coxed four and punch him repeatedly in the face when he wasn't rowing hard enough. Often by the end of the rowing session his nose would be completely bloodied. I'm not advocating this training technique for any parents who might be reading this, but I can tell you that Haining went on to be a three-time lightweight world champion.

My own upbringing was less dramatic, but still one in which abuse definitely played a role. My small size, coupled with a snarky attitude, seemed to invite hostile behavior. My presence was like blood in the water for the playground sharks.

"I'm going to get you, Boyne," became an all-too-familiar refrain, generally uttered right after the Pledge of Allegiance at the start of each day.

In a perverse sort of way, I felt quite popular. Certainly I would have preferred to remain a little more anonymous, but sarcasm seemed to fly off my tongue with the ease of a second language. My second-grade teacher, Mrs. O'Halloran, frequently kept me after school for blurting out inappropriate things, and eventually she theorized that I wasn't entirely human, but more of a changeling—exchanged at birth by the fairies. I almost believed her, for the shape and pitch of my ears lent me the aspect of an elf.

Human or not, there was something about me that incited reprisal, and it was not restricted to the male gender. During my first week of third grade in a brand-new school system, I was set upon by Tina Botigliere, a Russian girl whom I'd made the mistake of sitting next to on the school bus. Apparently this wasn't done; no one sat next to "Big Tina." The reason only became obvious to me after I sat down beside her and realized that Tina seldom bothered to shower. It seemed rude to switch seats, however, so I held my breath as long as I could and tried not to wince—a technique that I often used when served sauerkraut for dinner. Tina took one look at me, squirming uncomfortably in my seat, then leaned over and whispered, "I'm gonna have to beat you up, kid. But don't worry, then we'll be best friends."

True to her word, during afternoon recess Tina threw me down and sat on me in the playground. I'm pretty sure she wanted to kiss me, but she settled for pulling my hair and tugging my elf ears, perhaps to make sure they were real. Then for the rest of the semester, she insisted that I sit next to her on the way to school.

I'm not sure which torture was worse.

As time went by, I progressed to more garden-variety beatings. After making fun of Eddie Casner's sister in fifth grade, he and his buddies ambushed me after school, throwing me up against the brick wall before I could make it to the bike rack. They broke the first watch I ever owned, a gift from my grandfather. To be fair, Eddie had warned me to take off the watch, which was rather gentlemanly of him despite his thuggish nature. He also let the air out of my bike tires, but this was also a blessing, because it allowed me time to dry my tears as I walked home.

When I reached high school, I foolishly thought I'd be in the clear. After all, most of the career roughnecks had been dispensed with—sent off to reform schools or Outward Bound programs—and any bullies that remained had by and large sublimated their craft into verbal abuse. I could certainly handle that and give it back in return. Of course there were still occasional bareknuckle brawls in the school hallways, which the student body embraced, locking arms so that the teachers couldn't break them up. But mostly the hate that passed between rival groups and individuals displayed itself in a more subtle manner—the all-too-familiar juvenile put-downs that often make their way into the pages of young adult novels—pitting one clique against another: jocks against nerds, drama kids against jocks. The term *bullying* hadn't yet been assigned to this sort of behavior. Boys would be boys, and girls would be girls, and you learned to take abuse because it built character.

It was odd, then, when I was targeted by a football jock who longed to be a nerd—a "crossover clique" bully named Samuel Caluso. All through the lower grades he and his buddies chased me through the halls, often shouldering me against the lockers or threatening a "honey dip" if they caught me. Then, during our senior year, when everyone got serious and turned their sights toward higher education, Caluso tried to play the scholar-athlete card on his college applications in order to get into his dream school—Trinity College. But when the class rankings came out and I was listed as the salutatorian, several places above him, he was furious. To make matters worse, I'd already been awarded a varsity letter for cross-country running during my sophomore year, which he hadn't received in football until the year after. Without even trying I was considered a scholar athlete by most colleges—not that I thought much about those things. I'd taken up running mostly to get away from malicious people and exercised my brain to outwit them when the occasion called for it.

Caluso, of course, dismissed cross-country running as a sissy sport. When the class rankings came out, he actually stood up before our teacher arrived in calculus and delivered a lengthy soliloquy about how I didn't deserve to be ranked second in the class. Naturally I had to sit there and listen to this abusive blather, for I had no doubt that even with the recent judo lessons I'd taken at the YMCA, Caluso could have taken me apart with the same ease with which I took apart math problems.

Fortunately all things pass. High school, and the endless punishment of my senior year, finally ended. At last I was rid of my nemesis—or was I? So complete was Caluso's jealousy of me that after we graduated that spring, he began to pursue a girl I'd gone out with during the year—Mary Simmons. I'm not sure whether he even liked Mary, to be honest, but he seemed to crave everything about my life while at the same time taking every opportunity to denounce me. Mary and I had remained friends after we broke up, however, and during a recent conversation, she told me that Caluso had decided to go out for lightweight crew at the Coast Guard Academy.

Weird, I thought. Actually, double weird. Not many football players switched over to rowing, and fewer were able to suck down and row lightweight. Yet Caluso's fate was somehow entwined with my own for at least a little while longer.

After learning this information, I casually asked Coach Poole whether Coast Guard Academy was even in our league.

He nodded enthusiastically and said, "Oh yes, they're our arch rivals!"

CHAPTER THREE

This Boathouse Is Protected by Helios Rays

Ah, fall rowing and the innocent joys of novice crew—the long, technical rows in pairs, fours, and sixes; the leisurely pace that allows you to learn and refine your strokes; the ample downtime to look about and admire the changing foliage and appreciate the unique and timeless wonder of being out on a river, far away from the cares of the world and the trivialities of campus life.

Nowadays, much of this innocence has been lost, as the majority of U.S. collegiate oarsmen and -women are heavily recruited and quickly mainstreamed into varsity boats. But back in the 1970s, even at big institutions like Harvard and Yale, crew was primarily something you learned during your freshman year. Sequestered with a like-minded group of first-year classmates, you were shielded from the grim rigors that lay ahead. This permitted you to enjoy the slower, simple process of learning the sport without the urgency of producing an erg score.

Aside from a few guys who had been fortunate enough to row in prep school, the rest of us showed up at the Bliss Boathouse in a state of curious bewilderment, taking in the details of our new surroundings with hopeful, observant eyes. Most of us were simply dressed in baggy sweatpants and T-shirts, having not yet earned the right to wear a Trinity Crew splash jacket. Standing off to the outskirts of the boathouse, we respectfully watched the upperclassmen lift, shoulder, and launch their boats and listened carefully to Coach Poole's instructions in order to avoid messing up when it came our turn.

I was anxious, of course, but among this new group of novices, my slate was clean and I had the chance to remake myself. No one knew what I could do, including myself. Much to my surprise, no one had a superior attitude around the boathouse, due mainly to Norm Graf, the head coach and patriarch of Trinity Crew, who had instituted rules of protocol that inculcated respect and cama- raderie among all of the programs, women and men alike. Rumor had it that he came from a military background, and he did not tolerate disrespect. As freshmen we didn't have much direct exposure to Graf at first, but we felt his presence nonetheless— the hawklike stare that quickly took in the swirl of activity and the raspy, bellowing voice that echoed out on the river and within the boathouse bays. Back then, even at age fifty-two, Coach Graf was like some sort of mythical icon at Trinity, someone you learned to revere and fear in equal measure.

The Bliss Boathouse was a simple concrete brick struc- ture located on the outskirts of East Hartford. It was set on a dead-end road that looked like an abandoned industrial park, far enough away from campus that most people drove their own cars to get there, although a few brave souls ran, braving bad roads and sketchy neighborhoods. Yet even though the boathouse itself wasn't situated in the most bucolic section of the city, below it, down a steep paved grade, lay the ancient, ever-moving waters of the Connecticut River. The river was the longest and most impres- sive waterway in New England, and it was soon to become my gateway to another world.

"I wonder what that's supposed to mean," said another freshman standing next to me. He pointed to a small, official-looking sign perched in one of the boathouse windows:

Warning: This Building Protected by Dangerous Helios Rays.

Coach Graf, who had created the sign to ward off local vandals, had a wry sense of humor. Seeing us examining the sign, he suddenly veered toward us.

"What are you freshmen looking at?" he barked, with a twinkle in his eye and a barely concealed grin. "Get busy and take down your oars!"

Charlie Poole laughed and ushered us into the bays. He knew all about Graf's gruff exterior, having rowed under him for four years. Now it was his turn to coach, and he clearly wanted to do an equally good job. But as he looked over the roster and briefly did a roll call, a puzzled look came over Poole's face. It turned out that on that first day there were nineteen of us present with only eighteen seats available.

"Hmmm. Dan, why don't you take the single?" he suggested.

Shit, I thought. I'd been dreading this moment.

All eyes followed me as I carefully lifted the wooden shell off the rack and strode down the aluminum dock with it balanced on my shoulder. Few people on the entire team knew how to scull, and most were impressed that I knew how to carry the delicate craft. When I got down to the dock, I set it carefully into the water and fastened a set of Pocock oars into the old brass oarlocks. Then I gingerly lowered myself into the narrow cockpit, avoiding the novice mistake of stepping directly into the bottom. Holding both oars in my right hand, I took a deep breath and shoved off with my left. Fortunately a strong current immediately carried me downstream and well out of sight.

I took a few tentative strokes to avoid hitting the shore, and then started off with some easy drills to see how the boat would respond. My main goal, of course, was to make it out and back to the boathouse in one piece. As I slowly lengthened out to full reach, taking half and then three-quarter slide strokes to warm up, part of me began to worry that I'd catch a crab and get pitched into the swift waters of the Connecticut. That would put an abrupt end to my rowing career at Trinity. It would be dangerous, too, for I wasn't on little Roger's Lake anymore. I simply couldn't let that happen, so in lieu of a coach, I started swearing at myself:

You idiot! Why did you tell the coach that you knew how to row?

Because you wouldn't have made the team otherwise, an inner voice replied.

I must have appeared like a raving lunatic to the random seagulls and ducks, bobbing happily in the water nearby. As I kept cursing to myself, however, still anxious about flipping, my sculling became smoother as I drove my rowing demons away. The boat itself was a blessing; it forgave the small errors in my technique and gave me confidence as I continued along, making decent headway into the strong upstream current. At Blood Street I'd always been denied the beautiful wooden shells, which were reserved for the more experienced scullers. Their crappy old fiberglass trainers, ill-rigged and uncared for, hadn't done my nascent sculling any favors. This boat, however, was set up perfectly, and it responded dutifully even under my tentative hands. Soon I was zipping along, making decent speed. I went by one of the varsity eights, which had briefly "weighed enough" for a rest.

"Hey, who's the scrawny kid in the single?" I heard one of them say.

"Some frosh, light," another responded, disinterested.

"Not bad," came another.

"WELL, DO YOU KNOW WHAT I THINK ABOUT SCULLING?" shouted Mongo, the ogre-like upperclassman I'd met at the recruiting table.

He promptly issued a giant fart, which reverberated in the open fiberglass hull of the boat. Everyone laughed, including me, and I nearly lost my balance. Undaunted, I made it back to the dock, dry and happy, and safely put the single back into its berth without a scratch.

"Nice job out there," Coach Poole said. "Even the varsity heavyweights were impressed."

"Well, not all of them," I smiled.

"You mean Jowurski?" Charlie laughed. "Oh don't worry, you'll get used to him. He's kind of an acquired taste."

"That's for sure," I agreed.

Yet Mongo had definitely made a point, albeit in his own crude way. Sculling could be cool in a balletic sort of way, but sweep rowing was definitely more badass. A sweep oar was a massive piece of lumber, and it made you feel macho just carrying one around. Lacrosse players be damned, their little sticks were like flyswatters in comparison. And an eight-oared shell, nearly sixty feet in length, was like a waterborne juggernaut in the right hands, harkening back to the days of the Greek triremes. These were the musings of my first friend on the Trinity team at least, a nerdy upperclassman named William Windridge. He explained all of this to me (and much more) at dinner that evening:

"Even Archimedes, the designer of one of the largest of those ancient vessels, would have been proud of the modern rowing shell and the huge levers used to propel it. And let's not forget Teddy Roosevelt, whose fifth cousin Franklin rowed at Harvard. He clearly must have been thinking of the sport when he appropriated the African expression: Speak softly, carry a big stick, and you will go far."

Windridge was an odd fellow, both in appearance and manner. Erudite to a fault, his cropped brown hair and habit of constantly blinking lent him the appearance of a mole that had recently surfaced from underground. And every time he blinked, it seemed another thought occurred to him that he simply had to share. He didn't bother to put these proclamations in any particular order, or to assess the willingness of his audience to hear them. And when I tried to contribute to the conversation by making a point about sculling, he quickly cut me off:

"Sculling can be taken for leisure or sport, but rowing in eights is a serious business. And that business is to win races. This is probably due to the fact that the original crew competitions were held between Whitehall cargo vessels in New York and Philadelphia; they had fixed seats, of course, but the basic stroke mechanics were the same . . ."

Windridge prattled on, until I was barely listening.

Despite all of this historical hoopla, the fact was I had found the transition to sweeps quite challenging.

First off, the asymmetry and contortionism of the sweeping motion felt inherently wrong, after having started with an oar in each hand. And then, despite the promise of rowing on a team, Coach Poole quickly divided us into opposite camps—ports and starboards. How could that bipolar arrangement create anything but dissension? After all, each pair of oarsmen rotated away from each other at the beginning of each stroke, yet they were expected to follow each other. It reminded me of a sack race, where two people had to put one of their legs into a burlap bag and learn to run together.

Looking back, it is difficult to remember the first strokes one takes with any sort of clarity. They are like the first clumsy steps of a toddler, forgotten in the effort to merely stay upright. Because of my size, I was placed in the two seat, a position toward the bow, where balance and visual focus were a constant struggle. I found it no simple task to look at one guy's back for swing timing, and another guy's oar for a proper catch. Needless to say, these various challenges couldn't be mastered through book study and theory; they had to be experienced. Our novice crew wasn't a pretty sight at first, but fortunately our progress was fast and Charlie was quite patient with us, drilling us with the various exercises that Norm Graf had once shown him.

Meanwhile, there was no real pressure to perform; we were all simply having fun messing about in boats and enjoying the novelty of it all. In those days freshman fall crew was not a completely serious endeavor, but merely a testing ground to see who could tolerate the odd challenges of the sport—not the least of which was to endure the worsening weather that late September ushered in. Even so, as October began, we heard whispers that some of us would be chosen to row in a prestigious three-mile race in Boston coming up in three weeks' time. And as Windridge had implied, it was the incentive of being chosen for one of these competitive eights that kept us going as the days grew shorter and the less hardy souls began to disappear from practice, drifting off to less Spartan endeavors.

The name of the race, Windridge informed me, was the Head of the Charles Regatta.

CHAPTER FOUR

The Recalcitrant Coxswain

"Pull harder, you lazy b-bastards!" our coxswain shouted.

We were entering the last mile of the Head of the Charles, and by some small miracle no other boats had passed us yet. Cornell and Columbia were locked in a furious battle just off our stern, however, and it was only a matter of time before they would close the gap.

"C'mon, give me some real p-p-power! Make yourselves p-puke!" Phil said, in a sadistic, almost gleeful, tone of voice.

I'd made the frosh lightweight boat by the skin of my teeth, holding down the two seat of the bow pair with another lightweight named Tom Crowell. There are many advantages to rowing in the front of the boat, but there are challenges, too, particularly when you have a psychopathic helmsman and you're racing on a course strewn with obstacles including buoys, bridges, and other boats.

Philippe Poupé, our foul-mouthed cox, had gained his seat by default. Everyone else that Coach Poole recruited for that position had quit, unable to handle the rigors of morning practice. We were all praying that Poupé would follow suit. He was an insufferable soul who clearly hated coxing, and he had a jealous disdain for those of us who rowed.

Some coxswains are just plain mean, and like junkyard dogs you learn to stay away from them. But Poupé, who was the son of a prominent New York City art critic, could be clever and charming when he wanted to be, which made his derisive comments sting all the more.

"You guys row like old people have sex—slow and sloppy!"

It was impossible to tell whether this latest insult was directed at us or at our opponents, but it hardly mattered. The two Ivy League crews had now drawn even with our stern, and the middle arch of the Anderson Bridge loomed ahead, promising passage for only two eights.

As if on cue, Cornell began to advance on our starboard side, Columbia on our port. We were caught between Scylla and Charybdis, and Poupé knew it.

"Yield!" the Cornell cox called out, cutting inside of us.

"Move!" the Columbia cox demanded, swerving the other way.

Suddenly, thirty-two oars clashed together violently under the bridge, creating a terrible racket. The two other eights had essentially sandwiched us, bringing our novice Trinity boat to a complete halt.

"B-b-bugger off, you Ivy League a-holes!" Poupé shouted, as Cornell and Columbia trampled through us and just kept rowing.

I laughed, despite the absurdity of our situation, and then quickly regained control of my oar, which had been ripped out of my hands during the collision. We rowed on, undaunted, but I couldn't stop myself from smiling periodically. Despite his numerous faults, our fearless coxswain had an unassailable ego. Poupé even wore his speech impediment with pride, acting as if the rest of us were saddled with a more commonplace tongue. An eccentric dandy, he had a thick briar patch of black curls crowning his head, which he unsuccessfully tried to tame with hair product.

And much to Coach Poole's dismay, Phil refused to wear any sort of athletic clothing, preferring the black jeans and turtleneck garb of a beat poet.

Yet as much of a demon as he was in the coxswain's seat, once on dry land, Poupé was even more insufferable. After the race, when our boat was back in slings and our coach wasn't looking, he produced a packet of Gitanes from his back pocket and started puffing away, while the rest of us set to the task of de-rigging. After a long drag, followed by a slow pursed-lip exhale, he held the French cigarette within the folds of his long, delicate fingers and sneered at anyone who dared challenge him.

"Rowing is so d-damn asinine," he quipped, looking scornfully at the next race going by. "I really don't understand why people get so worked up about this c-crew crap anyway!"

"What do you mean?" I asked. I liked Phil for some strange reason and often hung out with him, just to hear what sort of villainous bile would come out of his mouth.

He rolled his dark eyes heavenward, as if the answer was obvious, then sneered with devilish delight. With his high cheekbones, rampant acne, and arched eyebrows, his face was an odd assortment of features that came together to form an exaggerated, artificial look—much like an evil mannequin in a B–horror movie.

"Oh my g-g-god!" he exclaimed. "Who in their right m-mind would want to wake up at a god-awful time in the morning and freeze their ass off just for this? C-christ, I'd rather be reading Proust and sipping a glass of scotch."

"So why do you do it, Phil?" I asked.

He shrugged, at a rare loss for words.

"Because my father told me to, I suppose. He gave me some character-building bullshit line of crap."

"Seems like you have plenty of character already," I observed.

Just then two of the other guys from our crew walked over, angry about the collision we'd had during the race.

"Nice job, Poopee," one of them said.

"Oh that's brilliant," Phil replied. "I mean, no one's ever called me that one before! Did you think of it all by yourself?"

"You little French bastard," the other said. "You cost us the race!"

"I'm Belgian, you jackass," Poupé snapped back. "And I didn't cost you anything. I coxed your damn race for free!"

The two oarsmen just stood there, shaking their heads in disbelief.

Poupé tossed his half-smoked cigarette into the Charles, then began to walk away, proud and undefeated.

"I'm going off to find a bar," he said, glancing over his shoulder. "I think I need that glass of scotch right now!"

"But what about training rules?" I called out.

"Screw that. Tell Charlie I quit," he said.

And so, heading into winter, we were once again without a coxswain.

CHAPTER FIVE

Big Bad Erg

How can winter training be anything but hell?

After all, when you take an oarsman off the water and place him on a rowing machine, it has much the same effect as removing a fish from its natural habitat. In both cases the life form in question starts to flop around spasmodically, and then it begins to stink. Most of the guys on the Trinity team washed their workout clothes only once in a while, trying to get the most mileage out of each shirt, pair of shorts, or sweatshirt. While outdoors, the pungent odor of a twice- or thrice-used article of clothing can be effectively dispersed by moving air, but within the confines of a gym, the atmosphere is much less forgiving.

There was one particular guy on our team who often smelled seriously overripe, and because of this and other reasons, he was given the nickname Porgy. This *nom de plume* had nothing to do with the popular musical by Ira and George Gershwin, but instead was based on a type of fish, also known as a sea bream—good tasting, but not particularly attractive or sought after by game fishermen.

Scott Sparks, Porgy's real name, was short and stout and possessed many of the physical characteristics of that aquatic creature, described by Wikipedia as a "deep-bodied compressed fish with a small mouth separated by a broad space from the eye." The nickname, in fact, fit him rather perfectly, and he accepted it with good humor. Yet because Scott was such a likable (and actually handsome) guy, none of us had the heart to tell him the true meaning of this moniker, but instead led him to believe that it did indeed come from the main character of *Porgy and Bess*.

Every deception has its downside, of course, and this one was no exception. After demonstrating his considerable benchpressing abilities in the weight room, Scott often beat his chest like Tarzan and then broke into song, belting out the verse: "OH BESS, YOU ARE MY WOMAN NOW!" We quickly grew to despise the verse, until one day he sang it during our change of guard with the women's team, which by rare coincidence had a member on it named Bessie McDonald.

Bessie blushed, as did Scott. Our afternoon was complete.

—◆—

After weights, and a short team run, we still had to do some technical work in the indoor rowing tanks, and then each take our turn on the Gamut erg—a torturous contraption that has now been banned from most crew programs. I personally loved the tanks, because it was here that Coach Poole was able to point out the main deficiencies in my stroke. I, in turn, was able to remedy these errors by cross-referencing myself in the two mirrors that were positioned directly in front of me and off to the side.

I confess to developing a certain amount of obsessive behavior with technique, as I had made it my goal to become the most proficient oar on the team, knowing I would never be the strongest. This quest for technical excellence may have cultivated a little vanity as well, induced by gazing at myself in the tank mirrors for long periods of time. But if this was the case, I was largely unaware of it.

To be honest, most male athletes are as vain as they are smelly, but from a practical standpoint, some amount of self-appreciation is as natural and necessary as body odor, and it is only those in close proximity who must suffer the consequences.

Many crew programs have now done away with indoor tanks, which are expensive and messy in their own right, and I believe this is unfortunate. Not only is it good to admire oneself to some degree, since it provides some of the motivation to work hard, but more significant, perfecting one's rowing form is arguably as important as learning to pull hard. Which brings us back to the Gamut erg, the one winter training apparatus that I am not sad to see fade from popularity. We had a nickname for it—the Vomit-O-Meter.

The Gamut ergometer was a primordial beast of a contraption. It looked like a big metal monster that had been created one weekend by an engineer in his garage, just for kicks, using welding tools and various bits and pieces that just happened to be lying about, including a cheap bicycle tachometer and an oversize clock repurposed from a photographer's developing room.

The only clue that the machine involved rowing at all was the sawed-off end piece of a wooden sweep oar. This protruded from a square metal sleeve, which was linked to a spring-loaded metal armature, suspended below the seat deck. When you pulled on the oar handle, the metal armature moved in tandem underneath you, pulling on a cable and making a distinctive *twacking* noise at the completion of every stroke. The cable in turn spun a heavy, horizontal gyroscope made of cast iron, whose revolutions were recorded by the tachometer and the mileage counter. The former gave you a rough idea of your relative speed, the latter racked up points that ultimately ranked you among your peers. Maximum points within a designated period of time were what you were shooting for, and the big clock was set manually, by positioning the minute hand and then clicking the on button.

Unlike the sleek looking ergometers of today, the Gamut erg also had a unique way of accounting for—and handicapping— different-sized oarsmen. A simple disc brake ran along the inside of the metal cylinder, to which a string and then a small "basket" were attached. The more weight you put in the basket, the more the brake would hinder the spinning gyro. Heavier guys and gals had to row with more resistance in order to equalize everyone's efforts based on body mass. It was an imperfect system, of course, as was the release mechanism of the stroke, which caused the oar handle to occasionally slam into your solar plexus, like a gut punch. But it was a system nonetheless, and to my knowledge no one ever bothered to make any serious refinements to the machine over the years.

Understandably, oarsmen dreaded their encounters with the Gamut much more than they do the CII today, because the machine was neither smooth nor forgiving. It was like a mechanical bull that you agreed to challenge, but soon regretted the decision. With the first few pulls of the oar handle, the entire device began to creak like a metal beast that did not want to be awakened. And once it started, you could not get off until you were queasy, weak-kneed, and defeated.

We were introduced to the Gamut on the very same day that Porgy sang his love song to Bessie McDonald. Our good humor quickly faded as we gathered around to watch the final painful moments of a varsity heavyweight oarsman completing a ten-minute ergo test.

"Uh-oh, look out. He's gonna hurl!" cried Mongo, who was standing on the sidelines watching with great interest.

The upperclassman, Steve Gibbs, got off the erg and stumbled forward like a wounded animal, unsteady on his legs. Then he suddenly doubled over and tried to vomit, but nothing came out—only a thick wad of spit dangled from his open mouth.

"Christ, it's only the dry heaves, Gibbers!" Jowurski said, visibly disappointed with his teammate's performance.

"You guys should've seen the chick that just left," he said to us. "She pissed all over herself!"

We looked at each other and then at the floor under the erg, searching for signs that this might be true. There were in fact small puddles around the base, but we assumed that these were created by sweat.

"Damn," he said. "You freshmen will probably shit your pants. Better put on your diapers!"

Mongo laughed hysterically and hobbled away. He had an odd, bowlegged stride, like a sailor who had been too long at sea.

And that was our introduction to the Vomit-O-Meter.

Truth be told, the Gamut erg was really built for hulks like Jowurski and not the tiny guys on our lightweight squad, who Mongo had recently dubbed "the little licker gang." Most of us could only handle three to four pounds in the basket, since our average weight was well under one hundred fifty pounds. Nevertheless, Coach Poole gave us each a turn, beginning with the two guys who had rowed before, Peter Tyson and Richard Malabre. They were the only true lightweights among us, weighing in at roughly 156 pounds, and they executed the six by two–minute pieces with more poise and dignity than Steve Gibbs, the upperclassman who had preceded them. Yet both, I noticed, went out quite hard at the beginning of each effort and slumped forward with exhaustion at the very end.

I had serious doubts about what might happen when it came my turn, for even after rowing all fall and lifting weights, I still only topped off at 142.

"Now, Dan, just see what you can do and don't worry about the numbers," Charlie suggested, removing some weight from the basket. "And remember not to throw your shoulders at the catch."

I grabbed the thick handle with my inboard hand and slowly drew it toward me—*clack-clack-clack-clack-clack*. Then Coach Poole reset the clock for two minutes.

"Ready all, row!" he said.

Unlike the others, I decided to go out steady for the first minute, which was always the way I'd run cross-country races back in high school. I was a pacer, saving my best effort for the closing sprint. Entering the last thirty seconds, I ramped it up.

"Good, really good," Charlie said, when I'd finished the first one. "Now let's see if you can do even better—just let loose a little and see what happens."

As if on command, I scored higher on my next piece, and on every piece after that. Instead of flagging, I simply grew stronger and stronger each time, harnessing the wave of optimism created by Poole. It sounds corny, but Charlie had a way of instilling positive energy and self-confidence so that you really wanted to make him proud and happy, and when the look of excitement came over his face, it was infectious. Minutes later my arms and legs felt like cooked spaghetti, and my mouth was bone-dry, but I stepped off the Gamut and walked away, feeling like I'd just ridden on the back of a dragon. I felt taller, somehow, and a bit high from the rush of blood through my veins.

My scores were not the best on the team, but they were right behind Tyson and Malabre, both of whom were bigger and much more experienced than me.

If this were a novel and not a true story, now would be the perfect moment to describe how I channeled anger into those erg pieces, using resentment and hatred toward my old demons as a way to drive myself. But in fact I did no such thing. With Coach Poole by my side, there was little room for hatred in my heart, but instead the hope of infinite possibility. I mention all of this because there are many coaches at the top level of rowing who choose to motivate their athletes in that other way—using anger, hatred, fear, and the threat of reprisal as the dark tools of their trade. Years later, when I started coaching myself, I would meet some of these men and women, many of whom were celebrated as the best in their field due to the results they produced. What is seldom measured, of course, is the long-term impact they have on young lives, not only on their physical well-being, but the other layers that lie underneath. What Poole passed along to us was something much different.

When we'd all finished our pieces, Charlie had a special announcement.

"Next week we will formally go into training," he said. "Which means, no one can touch a drop of alcohol until after the Dad Vails."

A collective moan issued from the group, for keg parties were practically a way of life on campus.

"But," he continued, "I have a special treat for you. To celebrate the start of winter training and the sobriety rules, tonight I'm going to have some old teammates of mine take you out to the Nutshell."

We all cheered, as the Nutshell was our favorite off-campus pub.

"These ex-teammates are coming into town, and it's kind of a Trinity tradition for the alums to go out drinking with you and tell you stories about the old days. Just remember that anything they tell you about me probably isn't true!"

———

I confess that I don't remember much from that evening, perhaps because of the amount of beer we consumed. I do remember one of Charlie Poole's teammates—a friendly giant of a man named Harry Graves, who showed up on campus in his naval whites and escorted us to the pub. (Graves would later become father of three outstanding Trinity oarsmen—Peter, John, and Tom, all of whom were Olympic-level athletes.) I've never been much of a drinker, but Charlie's old pals kept plying us with pitchers of cheap beer and stories. Needless to say, when I stumbled back to my dorm, I couldn't remember the Jarvis door code and ended up having to throw sticks at my window to wake up my roommate.

"Hey! What's your problem?" Jim asked, sleepy-headed and grumpy.

I shook my head, disoriented, and tried to speak.

"We did some erg pieces, and then we went out for beers, and . . ."

Suddenly I leaned over and vomited into a trash barrel.

"I don't think I ever want to drink again," I mumbled.

Jim came out and ushered me back to our room.

"OK, buddy," he said. "Time for bed. And let's put you on the bottom bunk tonight."

CHAPTER SIX

Heavies vs. Lights

In lieu of an adversary, we often create our own.

I've already mentioned that all the Trinity squads got along well, whether they were composed of men or women, frosh or varsity, heavies or lights—but of course this was a relative truth. It was about as accurate as if I said, "Everyone in our boat was best friends." In other words, it isn't pure hogwash, but it does require further clarification. As anyone who has ever rowed knows, a crew team is seldom a cohesive unit 24/7, despite all the mumbo jumbo written by advertising agents and Hollywood screenwriters wishing to romanticize rowing in the public eye.

So what's the real story?

As far as I can tell, an oarsman's truth is relative to his or her proximity to water. Put an oar in their hands, a boat below them, and that is when things start to get real. Tell them to shut up and row hard and stay in time with others, and then you begin to find out what really matters. Everything else, is, well, hypothetical and make-believe. And oarsmen seem particularly prone to fantasy and hyperbole whenever they are marooned on dry land.

"I pulled a massive erg this afternoon," Sam Bradshaw announced at dinner one evening, about a week before Christmas break. He was the red-haired cocaptain and stroke of the frosh heavyweights, and one of the strongest guys on the squad. His eyes quickly scanned the table to see if anyone was impressed by this random proclamation.

"Well, I took a massive dump this morning," Porgy offered.

The frosh lights chuckled in concert.

"I suppose that about sums you guys up," Jason Smith declared, talking through a mouthful of mashed potatoes. "After all, light-weights aren't real oarsmen."

"Now that's a load of crap!" one of our guys shot back.

"Yeah, we can kick your butts!" said Joe Rhineman, a normally soft-spoken guy from California. We all stared at Rhino, wondering what he was thinking and how we could ever make good on this boast.

"Ooooh, we're really scared!" Smith replied, continuing to shovel down mashed potatoes with a cocky smile on his face.

All the oarsmen sat together in the dining hall, but there were subgroups within the overall Trinity Crew program. Most friendships were based on personality, of course, but others were based purely on what boat you were in and where you sat within the crew. Bow four or stern four, engine room or coxswain—each had their own sense of solidarity and pride. Recently the frosh heavies and lights had begun to split off into their separate camps, with both groups competing for Coach Poole's attention. Poole was a former heavyweight, so his natural sympathies lay with that group, but we lightweights were set on proving our worth in whatever way possible.

And now Rhino had thrown down the gauntlet.

Winter training wears on everyone's nerves, as does the gray-scale of winter in general. Light deprivation is bad enough, but the absence of water adds another challenge for oarsmen—they essentially don't know what to do without it. And when you take rowers away from the rigid structure and soothing rhythm provided by an eight-oared shell, gliding along the surface of some water, they quickly begin to revert to the native savagery of land-locked individualism.

It's not a *Lord of the Flies* level of depravity, but pretty close to it.

As I've mentioned before, coaches can make use of the competitive aspects of human nature by either creating workouts that build team cohesion, or by pitting people against each other. A skillful coach will naturally balance these two modalities. Team runs were one attempt at the former enterprise, and the streets around West Hartford offered some decent running routes. During our first freshman team run, Sam Bradshaw quickly broke away from the pack, challenging the rest of us to keep pace with him. I hung back, just behind him, and studied his stride, trying to determine if his enthusiasm was sustainable.

After a minute went by, another lightweight sidled up next to me. His nickname was Wean and he had just joined the freshman team, having decided to give up wrestling.

"Did you run in high school?" he asked.

"Yeah," I said.

"Me too."

We ran side by side, stride for stride, for the next half mile, settling into the easy rhythm that experienced harriers know how to find. The total distance for the run was roughly five miles, and Coach Poole was waiting for us with a stopwatch at the finish line.

"So when do you want to pass this joker?" Wean finally asked me.

I laughed. "Let's take him in the last mile," I suggested.

My running partner reluctantly agreed, but I could tell that he was chomping at the bit.

Wean, whose real name was Mark Malkovich, was clearly an excellent, if impatient, athlete. No one knew where his nickname came from, but it fit him well, for he had an almost childlike side that often prompted him to utter nonsensical phrases whenever he was required to physically restrain himself.

"Balls. Balls. Balls!" he blurted out, and then repeated the words to himself, like some sort of weird mantra.

I glanced over and he just smiled back, not offering any explanation. I usually preferred to run in silence, but it was good to have the company, nonetheless, despite Wean's affectations.

Sam Bradshaw was strong, but like most heavyweights he was not ideally suited for running. The bigger you are, the more you have to carry, and Bradshaw had an overabundance of muscle. After a few miles this began to work against him. And when his pace finally began to wane, my new running companion and I made our move, sprinting by him without mercy.

"Hey guys, let's run together!" Bradshaw called out to us as we flew by.

"Screw that!" Wean spouted.

I started laughing and just couldn't stop. I got a side stitch eventually and had to slow down over the final half mile. Bradshaw was still far behind, however, chugging along with the other nonrunners who had by now caught up to him.

"Balls. Balls. Balls!" cried Wean, slapping my back as I finished.

"Totally," I said. "That was fun!"

"That was for the lightweights!" he crowed.

I smiled, even though I felt a little badly about sprinting past Sam, who was actually a decent guy despite his Eagle Scout affectations. It was, after all, supposed to be a team run. Then again, Bradshaw had gone out fast at the beginning of the run, issuing a challenge for everyone else to beat him. That, combined with his boastfulness in the dining hall, had made him a candidate for a comeuppance. To his credit, however, Sam took defeat well, shaking hands with us and promising to kick our butts on the next run. I suddenly realized that Bradshaw was simply doing what a good stroke should do—pushing himself in order to push everyone else harder.

As I stood there waiting for my other teammates to come in, I couldn't help but think about the other Sam in my life, my old high school nemesis, Samuel Caluso. I wondered how he was doing at the Coast Guard Academy and what sort of training they were going through off-season. I realized I wanted to beat him so badly that I had connected him to Bradshaw in my mind simply because their first names were the same and they were both a little cocky. The desire to win was driving me along, and I could feel it like a dark force running through my veins.

Winning definitely does something to your brain, and like sugar it injects you with an instant high. On the downside, however, it can also leave you hungry for more and override your sense of goodwill toward your fellow man—especially when he stands between you and the finish line. Winter training, too, does something to your state of mind. Despite its obvious health benefit, all the working out we were doing was having its own downside. While weight lifting, running, and erging were certainly adding heft to my major muscle groups, they were also adding to the density of my gray matter. It could have simply been that I had less time to hit the books and exercise my brain, but by eight o'clock in the evening I was more or less useless for anything requiring much concentration.

Unless, of course, it concerned the opposite sex.

Chapter Seven

A Woman of Substance

With the exception of a few local dives like the Nutshell, the social scene at Trinity was mostly limited to on-campus options. When I wasn't working out, I followed the rest of the undergraduate herd and traversed the well-worn paths between the dining hall, the dorms, and occasionally the art cinema. It was a woefully circumscribed life, but then again most colleges are built to that end—designed for the purpose of keeping students insulated from the real world and trapped within their walls like captive sheep. Hartford, Connecticut, offered little respite from this monastic existence. A city that had once been one of the richest in the nation, and home to the celebrated author Mark Twain, had become in modern day "the insurance capital of the world."

Needless to say, it was not a cultural Mecca.

As a result, on the weekends, the half-dozen Greek fraternities on campus reigned supreme, despite attempts by college administrators to hold "semiformal" gatherings as alternatives to those dens of iniquity, whose floors reeked of cheap beer. The frat houses were by and large inhabited by oversolicitous upperclassmen who stood around like vultures trying to convince freshman guys to join their ranks and freshman women to share their beds.

As far as I was concerned, I had already joined one fraternity, the Trinity Crew, and that was enough. Aside from the high-brow castle of Saint Anthony's, sitting alone at the top of Mount Vernon Street, most of these residences were unimpressive from any perspective—architecturally or otherwise—and they diminished in quality the farther downhill you traveled. This was generally the direction that everyone went on a typical Saturday night, progressing from one house to the other, like trick-or-treaters.

The official Trinity semiformals were equally sad affairs. Since no one knew exactly what *semiformal* meant, people showed up in all manner of garb, including leisure suits—an unfortunate fashion choice during the final days of disco in the late 1970s. Most of us freshman guys stood around like a bunch of stiffs, waiting for the lights to dim. Eventually, a few brave souls among us ventured out onto the dance floor and shuffled to the sounds of Earth, Wind, and Fire; Donna Summer; or the Bee Gees. An hour or so was about the length of time you could tolerate such abuse—then it was off to the frat parties to try your luck.

Naturally I made liberal use of my membership on the crew team to gain entry into those private establishments, whose weekend fetes were often restricted to "members and their guests only." Psi U and AD both had varsity oarsmen among their ranks, and one could easily cop a free beer by chalking it up to an unsuspecting brother—particularly if he was away that weekend. I also tried to use my nascent rowing membership as social currency with the opposite sex. After all, most anyone who didn't row seemed impressed by the sport, and one evening at Psi U's Polynesia fete, *Kamanawanalaya*, I caught the ear of a beautiful Iranian girl who seemed quite captivated by my descriptions of the Connecticut River.

"Tell me more about this—ROwing," she said.

Her name was Kooshe, and her awkward use of English only added to her charm, as did the numerous bracelets on her forearms. They slid up and down and chimed together as she moved, creating a musical accompaniment to all of her gestures.

"Well, rowing crew is intense . . ." I started to explain over the din.

Suddenly I heard a familiar voice come tumbling over my shoulder, repeating my words like an annoying parrot.

"*Rowing crew?* Excuse me, but you don't *row* crew," William Windridge corrected. "That sentence construction is improper."

He had been standing behind me, eavesdropping on my conversation, along with Mongo, who stood right next to him, grinning like an idiot. Both of them were wearing short-sleeve Hawaiian shirts and khakis, with plastic leis slung around their necks. Crew people are good at many things, but social interaction and fashion are not high up on the list.

"Whatever, Windridge," I said, trying to give him the brush.

"It's not '*whatever*,'" Windridge pressed on. "As a novice, it's important for you to learn the proper terminology."

"That's right, knucklehead," Mongo chimed in. "It's an oxymoron."

"I really don't care . . .," I said, turning my back on both of them. I tried to recapture the attention of my female companion, but their presence made this all but impossible.

"It's not an oxymoron, actually," I heard Windridge mutter to Mongo. "It's simply a redundancy."

"Well, you're an oxymoron, Windridge, and now I'm going to kick your ass!"

Mongo chased Windridge out of the frat hall. I admit that I'd never seen either one of them move that fast; they were usually the slowest on the team runs.

Immediately a spirit of combativeness seemed to catch hold in the room. Kooshe and I watched as a wrestling match spontaneously erupted between Wean and Jason Smith. Wean was fierce in battle, but Smith handled him with gentle authority.

"You know you're not going to win this one," Jason chuckled, as the two of them dropped onto the beer-stained floor, locked in an awkward embrace.

No one else moved or took much notice. Kooshe, however, lifted her dark eyebrows with great interest.

"Are these rowing friends of yours always so crazy?"

"Well, sometimes . . .," I tried to explain, apologetically.

"Oh, I like it. I think I should very much like to join this group," she said.

"Really?" I said.

"Yes!" she nodded.

"Well, OK . . .," I said.

She frowned. "You don't believe that I'm serious?"

"No, it isn't that," I said. "It's just—."

"Maybe you would like to arm wrestle with me, to see how strong I am?"

I almost spit up my ginger ale, and then I broke into an uncontrollable bout of hiccups. While the prospect of holding hands with this beautiful girl was enticing, an arm-wrestling match was not exactly what I had in mind. By this time, however, Mongo and Windridge had returned, having worked out their differences.

"C'mon, you wimp! Are you afraid of losing to a chick?"

I shook my head dismissively, as the memory of Big Tina began to emerge from the dark recesses of my brain.

"I'll officiate," Jason Smith offered, leading us over to a table.

Before I could object, Kooshe and I had locked hands, her bracelets jangling lightly. She bit her lower lip to prepare for battle and then stared intensely at me with deep-brown eyes.

I confess that I melted right then and there.

Guys generally know all the tricks of arm wrestling, like keeping a firm wrist by quickly curling it in. But Kooshe was a formidable opponent, and I found that I could not move her an inch, try though I might.

The match was already over, I just didn't know it yet.

"What are you waiting for, Boyne?" Mongo chided. "Take her down!"

Suddenly a beer was thrown in my face, blinding me, and then I felt my knuckles get slammed down violently.

"The winner!" Jason Smith said, holding up Kooshe's arm. I saw the two of them exchange glances, and then Kooshe beamed. I suspected foul play, of course, but there was nothing to do but grin and bear it. As I wiped the beer from my face, one thing became clear. I had just lost a potential girlfriend to Trinity Crew and quite possibly to Jason Smith. Fortunately my embarrassing loss was upstaged by the arrival of a newcomer clumping noisily down the stairs.

"Now what do we have here—a new recruit?" said the unmistakable, faux-military drawl of the women's varsity stroke, Cynda Davis. She was built like a bricklayer, with muscular arms and legs, and a mop of brown hair cut short like a boy.

"Oh Jesus," Mongo said. "It's Davis. Cop ya later!"

Apparently I wasn't the only one with a story to tell.

Chapter Eight

Sisters

As I've already mentioned, my sister Shawn was also rowing on the Connecticut River, some fifty miles upstream at Mount Holyoke College in South Hadley, Massachusetts. The same body of water and the same sport connected us, and it was because of her that I had picked up an oar in the first place. Of course it wasn't the only time that my older sibling had dragged me into an activity that I never would have otherwise pursued on my own.

When we were younger, I was more inclined to lay around listening to old Beatles songs and learning to play them on my guitar; Shawn was always in motion. A consummate tomboy, she could not stomach my artistic bent, which generally led me toward more solitary pursuits—most of which did not involve her. Athletes, of course, require playmates. And having witnessed my early defeats at the hands of various bullies in our neighborhood, she took it upon herself to toughen me up, engaging me in all manner of athletic endeavor. These activities were ostensibly designed to cultivate my manliness; but, of course, the prime objective was to keep her company.

This plan not only included pickup games of football, baseball, and basketball, but also spontaneous and less-structured methods of combat. Often, while I was innocently reading a superhero comic book, she would pounce on me like a crazed psychopath come to life from the pages of my favorite reading material, delivering a volley of punches, kicks, and karate chops. If these weren't sufficient to rouse me from my natural indolence, she would execute some sort of elaborate wrestling move she'd witnessed on TV. And so, in a weird sort of way, I wasn't too disturbed by my recent arm-wrestling loss to the Persian Princess, as Kooshe became known, for I'd grown up constantly being challenged by Shawn with these sorts of tests. I'd also learned to become more circumspect about what women could or couldn't do, the upshot being that I didn't really respect any girl who wasn't sporty to some degree. Still, it didn't mean that I wasn't disappointed by Kooshe's rejection of me in favor of the rowing team.

I tried to put the entire arm-wrestling episode behind me, but the next day in the dining hall the embarrassing tale was tossed about from table to table like a piece of rotten fruit. Eventually it landed back in my lap, where I had to sit and listen to my own teammates discuss my defeat with great relish, eventually launching into various theories about the unpredictable nature of the opposite sex. Most of the guys did not have girlfriends yet, so these discussions were largely speculative in nature due to a lack of actual field experience.

While most of them concluded that I had failed miserably on all fronts, our newly elected captain, Richard Malabre (alias Dak), had a different take.

"Women make you docile," he said, in a deep matter-of-fact voice.

This sober, almost biblical judgment silenced all conversation at our table, as if it struck a true chord deep within our young male psyches.

But only for a nanosecond.

"That's bullshit," said Rob Leavitt, who was studying premed.

"Yeah, women get you jazzed," said Porgy, grinning.

I remained largely silent, feeling fortunate that the conversation had shifted away from me and into more productive fields of gossip.

"Hey, did anyone get the skinny on Cynda Davis?" Wean asked.

I shook my head, as did everyone else.

Rumors had been circulating about a one-night tryst between Davis and an unnamed varsity male oarsman. No details had emerged, but I'd witnessed how Mongo had suspiciously fled from the frat party upon her arrival. Then again, another varsity oarsman named Edward Noman had recently confessed to blacking out in a drunken stupor and then waking up beside one of the varsity women on a sofa at AD. Totally embarrassed, he had quickly grabbed his clothes and skulked away. As freshmen we were only privy to bits and pieces of gossip like this, since most of the varsity oarsmen didn't want to reveal anything too incriminating— material that might come back to haunt them at Skit Night, held during the upcoming spring break in March.

Now that we were off the water, in fact, I'd begun to discover that there was quite a bit of inter-squad dating among oarsmen and -women, some of which worked out well and some not. Our own coach, Charlie Poole, ended up marrying a former Trinity coxswain, a not uncommon occurrence in the crew world. For whatever reason, though, I had no interest in this sort of thing, which seemed a little too close to home. Perhaps, too, it explained why I had reacted with some reserve when Kooshe revealed her desire to join the team—not because of any moral high ground, but because I suspected that things could get messy with rowing romances.

What I didn't realize about the women's team, however, was that this year was to be something of a landmark in their short history.

Only a few years prior, the first Trinity women's crews had been launched, despite some absurd fears that they might create a potential distraction for the men's team. Initially they were required to practice only in the early morning and only during the fall season. By the time I arrived, however, things had changed. Head coach Norm Graf had realized their true potential as dedicated athletes who might make a significant contribution to the team. The squads were now intermingled, and this year's group would be the first to row through the spring and compete at the National Championships in Philadelphia. If the men and the women both did well, Trinity would have a shot at the combined points trophy awarded to the college with the most top finishers.

—◦—

Not long after dinner, I decided to go run stairs in order to clear my head. Stair climbing is a lonely endeavor, but I'd eventually discovered that the simple act of counting steps, flights, and the number of ascents could provide an immediate sense of accomplishment. At Trinity we had access to the eight-story concrete fire exit steps at the High Rise dorm, although they lacked the benefits of clean, fresh air. The dryness quickly made your lungs and legs burn. And then there was the practical problem of having no place to spit, which meant that many of us simply let loose wherever it was convenient, much to the dismay of the building residents.

As I came back down from my third ascent, I suddenly heard the bottom door slam, and then the unmistakable sound of another athlete beginning to ascend the stairs below. I immediately picked up my pace and braced myself for battle. Sam Bradshaw often trained at the same time as me, and there was no way I was going to let him pass me. But as I descended, I came face-to-face with a young woman I hadn't noticed before, wearing a crew jacket. She had a vaguely familiar Scandinavian look, bobbed hair, and an unusually composed demeanor considering the physical activity we were engaged in. As we passed one another she said, "Hi," in a deep, resonant voice that reminded me of an actress or jazz singer.

We continued up and down the flights, crossing paths midway several more times, smiling and encouraging each other on. I did twelve flights that night, a personal record for me, and I stopped when my running companion completed her last set. As it turned out, she lived in the same dorm as me, so after we finished, we walked back to the quad together in the dark and chatted about the challenges of freshman crew. Like me, she was relatively new to the sport and wasn't sure how she would do because she wasn't that big. She had an easy way about her that was not typical of Trinity, or of New England in general, and I was not surprised to learn she was from Wisconsin, where I'd been born. As we parted ways, it finally struck me why she seemed so familiar: With her short brown hair and winsome smile, she reminded me of my sister.

Her name was Heidi Wittwer, and she was to play a role on our freshman lightweight team that no one could have predicted.

CHAPTER NINE

Celibacy

I haven't mentioned much about the Trinity campus, other than the dorms, the fraternities, and the dining hall, but of course the other place where students congregated was the college library, mostly because we were all expected to put in our time there. The main area was commonly known as the fishbowl. I'm not sure whether it was the stale air, or the smell of old books, but to me the stone edifice felt more like a mausoleum, and it seldom failed to put me straight to sleep. I was surprised then, as I searched for an open study cubicle, to find Porgy attentively reading a huge Russian grammar textbook. I almost didn't recognize him with his glasses on.

"*Psst*. Hey, Porgy, what are you doing?" I asked him.

"What do you mean? I'm studying of course!"

"Really?"

"Yes, really," he said, momentarily displaying an offended frown—then he smirked.

"Actually, this is the perfect place to pick up girls," he whispered. "They love it when you look all studious and stuff."

"Seriously?"

He nodded. "I think it plays to their nesting instincts and makes it seem like you might be successful later on in life."

"That's a joke," I said.

"Totally, but it works," he replied. "You just have to be careful that you don't come off too confident or smart. It helps to ask them questions about homework assignments."

I shook my head in disbelief, suspecting that Porgy was simply conning these so-called girlfriends of his into doing homework for him. Nevertheless I took a seat nearby to observe whether the technique actually worked. I'd been having very little success on the dating front myself, now that drinking rules were in play and parties were out. I was also a little gun-shy after my last outing, when I'd been humiliated by Kooshe, the now-legendary freshman recruit.

Sure enough, after only a few minutes, a cute girl from our biology class wandered over and started chatting with Porgy. Soon a friend of hers joined them, and the trio started carrying on so loudly that someone nearby had to shush them. As the two young women placated the annoyed party in muted tones, Porgy glanced over at me and winked. Then I saw one of the girls write down something on his notebook that I assumed were the answers to his homework. When they'd left, I got up and went back over to his cubicle.

"Bingo!" he said.

"Bingo what?"

"I got their phone numbers!" he said, tapping the upper left corner of his notebook.

"Unbelievable," I said, shaking my head.

Porgy just bit on the end of his pen and smiled.

I returned to my cubicle, and for several minutes I attempted to try out the technique myself, without success. It could have been that I lacked faith in it, or I didn't have Porgy's knack for looking pleasantly stupefied by the problem sets in front of him. Some people are just naturally suited to be library lizards, and I wasn't one of them. At one point a girl from my German for Reading

Knowledge class breezed by and tossed me a promising glance, but when I tried to hail her down, she didn't bother to stop.

"*Beschaftig*," she said, glancing over her shoulder.

Schiesse, I replied, under my breath.

Porgy noticed my failed attempt and chuckled. Frustrated, I finally got up and walked out into the cool winter air. I was feeling restless, so I made my way in the direction of the field house, where my roommate Jim was just finishing a basketball game against Bates College. I'd never actually seen him play, despite numerous promises that I'd made and broken. Basketball was about the furthest sport from my wheelhouse, but I'd taken a mild interest in it for Jim's sake, and tonight he'd also promised to introduce me to his long-term girlfriend, now attending Bates.

All semester long Jim had also been telling me about his rivalry with a guy who'd graduated from Canton High School with him and then gotten into Trinity. They'd both made it onto the varsity basketball squad—Jim played forward and Roger played center, although they weren't much different in terms in height. Roger was just a bit beefier and more aggressive than Jim. I watched as he muscled his way under the hoop, grabbing the rebounds, while Jim held back a bit and carefully chose his shots. You wouldn't know the two were rivals from the way they played together on the court, and several times I saw Jim feed the ball to Roger so that he could take an easy layup.

Basketball was such a contrast to crew, with everyone constantly switching directions and effecting elaborate strategies that seemed to change by the moment. In crew there was really only one objective and that was forward momentum. Basketball was certainly much more exciting to watch than a crew race, and at the close of the game, Trinity had beaten Bates by eleven points. After the game, however, Jim looked pretty down in the mouth, considering that his team had just won.

"I can't believe it. She just broke up with me," he said, before I could even ask what was wrong.

He showed me the "Dear Jim" letter, which he'd obviously folded and unfolded numerous times. It was the standard sort of dismissal: "I still care about you but I've met someone else. I still want us to be friends . . ."

"That's pretty rough," I agreed.

We walked in silence for a while, heading back toward Jarvis.

"I have an idea," I said, as we walked under the Bancroft Arch passing into the main quad. "Let's check out the Cinestudio and maybe catch a film. You can drown your sorrows in a bag of popcorn."

"What's playing?" he asked glumly.

"*The Rocky Horror Picture Show.*"

"No thanks," Jim said. "I think I'll just pack it in and order a pizza."

Abandoned, I walked around the quad a little bit longer, then lingered under the Bancroft arch under Seabury Hall, where I stopped briefly to admire the carved wooden relief of an eight, donated by the class of 1938. It was a classic design that made rowing look iconic and ancient, especially placed under the archway like a cave painting. I thought about Jim for a while, and about the overall challenge of having a real relationship in college, especially as an athlete.

Suddenly a familiar voice called out, "Hey, Boyne!"

It was Phil Poupé, our ex-coxswain, walking arm in arm with two girls. They were all on their way to the Trinity Pub and already in high spirits.

"Join us for a beer!" Phil said.

"Sorry, I can't," I said. "I'm in training now."

"Too bad!" he chuckled, arching his eyebrows and tilting his head left and right at his two companions.

"Yeah, it's kind of boring," I admitted.

"Well, ladies, it's a cold night, so huddle in close if you want to keep warm."

They laughed and strode off toward the pub. There were definitely some downsides to rowing that I hadn't counted on.

When I got back to my dorm, Jim was there, drowning his sorrows with a large pizza and a six-pack of beer.

"How are you doing?" I asked.

He shrugged and groaned a bit, like a wounded bear.

"Oh, by the way, some weird guy called for you," he said, pointing at a scrap of paper with a phone number scribbled on it. I looked at it curiously, noticing that the first three numbers were 669, the same ones for my hometown. It was late, but I picked up the phone and dialed the number just in case it was an emergency.

"Hello," I said. "This is Dan. Did someone call me from this number?"

"Yes," a deep, flat voice answered. "Is this the young man who is interested in joining the priesthood?"

"What?" I replied. "Who is this?"

"Father Francis, from St. Mary's Church. Your mother seemed to indicate at Sunday Mass last week that you might have an interest in pursuing theology."

I paused for a second and took a deep breath.

"Well, I am interested in theology," I said. "But I'm afraid that I have no interest in joining the priesthood. Sorry to waste your time," I said, and hung up.

Jim just looked at me and started laughing hysterically. I'd finally found a way to cheer him up.

Chapter Ten

Musical Chairs

I could feel their eyes on me, watching every stroke I took.

Dak, Pete Tyson, Wean, and I were rowing together in the tanks, working on the finer points of the stroke. Charlie Poole was standing below us, occasionally offering bits of advice, and beside him stood head coach Norm Graf. Every once in a while, glancing out at my oar, I could see them conferring, trying to puzzle something out. Although I took it for granted at the time, it was a weird thing to be watched constantly—particularly in a rowing shell, where one is held captive not only within a restricted area, but also within a limited and repetitive field of motion. In a way a coach is like a spy who witnesses your every move, putting you on guard but often making you perform better.

"OK, weigh enough," Charlie said. "Dan, switch places with Dak and move up to the stroke seat."

The words instantly brought excitement and fear into my psyche.

Dak and I got up and dutifully changed places. He was a much stronger oarsman than me and had much more right to occupy the lead seat.

In the fall Dak had served as our stroke, and together with Pete Tyson sitting right behind him in the seven seat, they had done a great job. This preliminary choice for the stern pair made a lot of sense, given the prior experience that these two brought from Exeter and Haverford. But now some of the more novice oarsmen like myself had gained more competence, and with spring approaching, Charlie needed to reconsider the lineup. We'd also lost a few strong lightweights that winter and gained a few new ones who'd never rowed at all. One was a guy we simply called Tex, because he was from Texas; the other, Henry Phillips, was the son of a Trinity chemistry professor.

All told, there were now nine of us competing for eight seats and still no coxswain to be found.

It is perhaps more of an art form than a science to find the right combination of oarsmen in a crew that makes a boat go well. Naturally the stroke is of primary importance, as this person not only sets the cadence for the group but is also the one in whom everyone places his trust. I felt totally unprepared for this lead role, but that afternoon as we started paddling again with the new lineup, the coaches seemed to like what they saw. I had a natural sense of rhythm, balanced with a lot of patience on the slide. Clearly, all that guitar playing had paid off.

Charlie got out his stroke watch and called out some target ratings. I hit them intuitively almost every time.

"Nice job!" he called out. I glowed inside, but part of me was still uncertain.

It is one thing to be able to set a cadence, and quite another to be able to maintain it under pressure. To be sure, I was flattered, because sitting in the stroke seat is clearly an honor that dubs you as one of the better oarsmen in the boat. All rowers should try stroking at least once. When they do, they might discover that it is a lot like being handed the leadership of a company, or perhaps a small country; but it comes with a great responsibility that few people can handle.

For a week or so, I enjoyed my reign. There is a wonderful and true sense of power when everyone falls into line behind you, and you feel the collective crush of oars against still water. Out on the river, as our boat surged forward, my own single oar seemed to carry the authority of seven others. For a while I felt like a superhero, just like the ones in the comic books of my youth. We had just started to get back on the water a few times a week, as the winter ice broke up and the weather brightened. Everyone was quietly optimistic.

Then steadily, I began to get tired.

At first I thought it was the cold doing me in, as it became harder and harder for me to get out of bed each morning. Then one day, sitting at stroke, I suddenly realized what was wrong. With no one else to follow, I never had any time to relax. My catches grew stale, and no matter how many times Charlie reminded me to "drop the blade right in," I started hesitating at the start of each stroke, as if I were waiting for everyone else. Ironically, all the control I possessed began to work against me, and I started to get worn down, trying to second-guess whether I was setting the right pace. I even dreamed about it in my sleep, and occasionally it woke me up at night.

When Charlie finally pulled me from the seat, I was actually a little relieved. Next he tried out Henry Phillips. Like myself, Henry was lanky and lean and had a decent stroke for someone who had just learned how to row. His main problem, however, was that no one accepted him. He wasn't a bad guy, really, he just had no racing experience whatsoever, not even the past fall, and his erg scores were some of the slowest on the squad.

"Look at how skinny his legs are," Rob Leavitt griped.

"Yeah. And did you see how he dropped out on the last team run?" Porgy added.

With these few words the beginnings of mutiny had commenced.

Eventually Coach Poole saw that no one would follow poor Henry. Chaos reigned for a few days, and then he, too, was relieved of command. And so, heading into March, we were not only uncertain about who could handle the stroke seat, but also who was going to steer our boat. And as the ice finally melted completely and we took to the Connecticut River more regularly, Charlie began a game of musical chairs. Each day one of us would cox so that the rest of the team could practice, and everyone on the port side got a chance to stroke. More often than not, Tex ended up as our cox'n, for he had a propensity to crab with such violence and frequency that we secretly began to refer to him as King Crab. He was simply not cut out for rowing, which is a rare thing indeed.

Then one day, just before spring break, Charlie announced that he had a surprise for us, as we piled into his station wagon that served as the team bus.

"It took me awhile, but I think I've figured out a good lineup," he said.

At the boathouse we drifted into the bays and found our eight laying right-side up in slings. Something looked weird about it. The stroke seat rigger had been moved to the starboard side, and behind it were two consecutive port riggers.

"It's called a bucket," Charlie explained. "European crews use them a lot."

"Very cool," Wean remarked.

Peter Tyson was selected as the starboard stroke, followed by me and Henry Phillips in "the bucket." Dak, the strongest and biggest of us all, was installed in the five seat. The bow four consisted of Joe "Rhino" Rhineman, Rob Leavitt, Porgy, and Wean.

Everyone seemed relatively happy about the new lineup, but a few things were clearly missing.

"Where's Tex?" Rob Leavitt asked.

"You mean King Crab?" Wean muttered.

The bow four snickered.

Charlie shook his head and then politely announced that Tex had voluntarily dropped out. We were quiet for a second and suddenly felt ashamed.

"On a more positive note, I have another surprise for you," Charlie added, nodding over toward the entry of the boat bay, where we could hear the arrival of the other squads.

Everyone turned and watched as a familiar figure walked slowly forward and stood beside Charlie, all bundled up in winter coxing gear.

"Heidi just got cut from the women's team, but she's agreed to try out coxing for you guys—so be nice!"

We all looked at each other, secretly delighted.

"Balls-balls-balls. Seeds-seeds-seeds. Cubes-cubes-cubes!" Wean blurted out.

"What did he say?" Heidi asked.

"I think that means he likes you," I said.

Everyone laughed, and the ice was broken.

"All right then, boys—HANDS ON!" Heidi said, with a playful confidence and a smoky timbre to her voice that was kind of sexy.

Needless to say, she had our attention from the first command.

CHAPTER ELEVEN

Blind Faith

Charlie Poole had the rare gift of making every guy on our team believe that his position in the boat was not only unique but indispensable, and Heidi quickly picked up on this vibe. "Remember, you can catch more bees with honey than with vinegar," I heard him mention to her, as the rest of us laid "hands on" and then carried our boat down to the water to try out the new lineup again. Already, after the first few outings, I suspected that Charlie had chosen our seating plan well, distributing us along the eight in the positions where we would best contribute to the boat's speed and stability. Everyone felt it, and there was a new sense of confidence and excitement within the boat. Now it was just a matter of fine-tuning the eight-cylinder engine.

The spark plug, of course, was the ninth and newest member of the crew.

A good coxswain is a rare thing. In addition to steering and piloting the crew shell, the cox is the intermediary between the coach and the crew and needs to be able to translate the energy and intelligence of the coach to the boat. It is a double agent's role, of course, and not an easy thing to do—to side with the team but also push them harder. Many coxswains take a terrier approach, simply barking out commands and immediately assuming control of everything and everyone. But Heidi was a Midwesterner and more genial in the way she chose to handle a bunch of freshman guys, even those of us who had not yet grown up.

"OK, let's warm up with the pic drill," she called out through her headset. "Stern four first."

"Bite me," Wean muttered under his breath, just loud enough for everyone except Heidi to hear.

"What did he say?" Heidi asked Peter.

"Nothing important," Peter told her. "Don't pay him any attention."

Nevertheless, having a woman in our boat definitely changed things. Most of us checked what we said a little bit, curbing our foul language, while others tried to show off and see what they could get away with, even calling out suggestions to our new coxswain-in-training. Heidi was good-natured about all of this, for she was still a little uncertain about her new role and how far into the boat her domain extended. She hadn't yet learned her main weapon, of course, which was that deep underneath all of our macho posturing lay the need to be told exactly what to do.

"OK, after you finish the warm-up, let's try doing some eyes-closed rowing," Charlie announced from his launch. The Connecticut River in March was a flat gray palate, mirroring the blandness of the sky. A few seagulls hovered in the air, but none of the other birds had yet returned from their winter sojourn.

"OK, eyes closed," Heidi called out, echoing Poole's command.

"Yeah, we heard him," Wean grumbled, loud enough for everyone to hear.

We'd never done this drill before, because we weren't ready for it yet. Rowing in an eight-oared shell initially requires a keen attentiveness to visual detail—not only what the other oarsmen in the boat are doing, but also the arc and pattern of one's own oar as it enters and exits from the water. There are a lot of moving parts to juggle, needless to say, and it takes time to filter out the unnecessary distractions that can beleaguer a novice, causing him to fall out of synch with the rest of the group. With eyes closed, many of these distractions were removed, but blindness required the development of a more subtle ability, commonly known as "boat feel." Like learning a foreign language, the ultimate key was repetition. Take a good stroke; then take it again. If things go wrong, fix it quickly and move on.

"Dan, no peeking!" Heidi said, catching me glancing out at my oar.

The eyes-closed drill was also supposed to make everyone in a crew learn to trust the boat as a whole. At first, however, as I gave into the exercise, I felt its primary values. Everything that was going on in my head suddenly dropped down into the lower half of my body, and instead of looking out at my oar, or the water, or Peter's shirt to get my bearings, I felt my connection to the seat and the hull of the boat. My tactile senses began to take over. I could feel the pulse and run of the boat, which guided my forward and back timing, and the left to right lateral balance. It was like developing a sense of sonar. If our crew had a group consciousness, it was clearly not in synch yet, but with each stroke forward, we were slowly finding it.

"OK, that's not bad," I heard Charlie call out. "Now let's try twenty strokes with eyes closed. Feel the boat run out underneath you, don't just focus on the drive."

"Eyes closed. Power twenty in three," Heidi echoed. "Build in one-two-three, here we go!"

After a few uncertain strokes where the boat briefly wobbled, our eight came together and found its center of balance. Rowing blind, I began to feel and hear more keenly the machinery of the boat working now—the clunk of the oars that preceded the catch, the sudden pulse of the drive, and the buttery glide of the shell as it carried us over the cold gray-green water.

"That's better!" Heidi said, excited. She told Charlie that there was less check between strokes, which could give a coxswain a case of whiplash. He nodded, satisfied with our efforts, and then started to motor away in order to work with the frosh heavies.

"Heidi, try another twenty," he said. "Then have them weigh enough and take their feet out of the shoes."

When Charlie had left, we tried another twenty with our eyes closed, then stopped rowing for a moment, in order to reset. When I opened my eyes again, the sun seemed more brilliant as it emerged from the clouds and sparkled in the broken water. Everything seemed more alive now, and our boat and the river felt less separate.

"OK. You heard Charlie," Heidi said. "Feet-out rowing."

"What?" Wean shouted from the bow. "That's crazy!"

"It's not crazy," Dak said. "It's an advanced drill. And if you don't know what you're talking about, keep your mouth shut!"

Wean grumbled but didn't dare question our captain.

We untied our shoes and set our feet on top of them, then started rowing again, trying out the new exercise. This one was a bit like riding on a horse without putting your feet in the stirrups, and now we had nothing to anchor us to the boat save the oars in our hands and the seats we sat on—both of which were in constant motion. I could hear the bow four, cursing under their breaths, as we unsuccessfully tried to learn how to C-shape our upper backs at the end of the drive, in order to counterbalance the layback. Done correctly "feet out" rowing taught you how to smoothly change directions out of the bow without tugging on the footboard, a novice mistake that could check the glide of the boat and slow it down substantially.

Just as we were all about to lose patience with the drill, Charlie motored back and sat just off our stern, watching us. His mere presence made us row better.

"Engage your stomach muscles—that's it, now. Careful, Rob, don't lift the legs too early!"

In rowing, self-confidence develops in tandem with boat skills, and as novice oarsmen we still had a shortage of both. Yet with each gentle correction and word of encouragement, our coach was slowly molding us into a real crew.

"That's it, Rob, hold those legs firm! And try to move your hands and shoulders forward when Rhino moves out of bow."

With his mop of black hair and bushy eyebrows, Rob Leavitt was the antithesis of Joe Rhineman, sitting right in front of him at four. Joe was phlegmatic, and Rob was hyperactive, yet by placing them together as a pair it somehow worked out brilliantly. The three seat was commonly viewed as the repository for an oarsman who simply couldn't be coached, but it was doubtful whether or not Rob knew this, or cared.

Nothing could rattle Joe, and likewise Dak, sitting one seat farther forward, at five, so between the two of them they effectively served as a buffer between the bow and the stern seats.

"Now Wean, don't set the catch quite so soon," Charlie continued. "I like your eagerness, but wait for Peter to put his blade in the water!"

I quietly chuckled at this comment, knowing that our bow seat sometimes believed he was stroking our boat from the front. Still, I found Wean's irreverence refreshing, for the most part, and I had a lot of respect for all the guys up in the bow. Theirs was not an easy job, as I'd learned from rowing in the two seat last fall. Back in the stern, Peter and I and Henry and Dak may have been the rhythm makers of our crew, but the bow four provided much of the balance for our boat, particularly Porgy and Wean.

I fixed my gaze on Peter's shoulders as Heidi called us into another power twenty, and together we slowly began to accelerate. I heard Charlie motor up next to us, directing his attention toward the stern four now.

"Dan, make sure to keep your blade square until it comes fully out of the water," he instructed. "Henry, same thing. Don't cut off the end of the stroke. Keep your outside wrists lifted as they come into your chest."

The seven seat suited my character well, for like Wean I had an innate resistance to being led, combined with an equally strong disinterest to lead. Sitting just one position back from stroke offered me the perfect compromise. I liked the fact that there was at least no other port oar in front of me—only a starboard. More-over, even though our stroke, Peter, provided the primary drum-beat for our crew, I was the "translator" of his enthusiastic efforts, much like the bass player in a jazz band.

"Three to build!" Heidi called out, boldly trying out some more power strokes with the feet out.

Peter wound it up again, and I followed—now feeling more than ever the pattern and rhythm of his stroke. Things were going along well. Then Heidi had us close our eyes again, and suddenly everything fell apart. Porgy fell backward, off of his seat. Rob crabbed. Henry jammed his oar handle into my back. The entire boat came to an ugly halt.

"Crap!" Rob yelled. "Porgy, you suck!"

"Bite me!" Porgy said. "It was Joe's fault."

"Was not!" Joe objected.

"This drill sucks," Wean concluded. "Heidi, why did you have us close our eyes with the feet out?"

"I thought you could handle it," Heidi shot back.

"OK, guys, that's enough," Charlie said, laughing. "Just relax. You can put your feet back in the shoes now and keep your eyes open, but here's the secret—try to pretend that you didn't do either!"

We started paddling again, and our rowing felt easier and more efficient now, as we took it back into the dock. The technical workout was over. After we'd put the boat away, everyone raced toward the new school minivan, fighting over the seats in the back. Heidi and Charlie came strolling up last and hopped into the driver and passenger seats. Charlie flicked the radio on, and the two of them fell into quiet conversation about the day's session. Meanwhile, in the backseats, we conversed about them.

"So what do we think of Heidi?" Joe said quietly.

"I think it's kind of weird having a girl in the boat," Rob remarked.

"I don't know," Porgy said. "I kind of like it. Besides, Heidi isn't really a girl, she's a coxswain."

"Hah-hah-hah," Wean laughed in staccato.

"That's a bit rude," Dak pointed out.

"But you know what I mean, though . . . most coxswains are like, well . . ."

"Asexual?" Peter suggested.

"Yeah, kind of. I mean, I guess she's not, really—but with all that gear on it's kind of hard to tell."

"How much does she weigh, anyhow?" Henry asked, who was only 137 pounds.

"Probably about as much as you!" Wean laughed.

"Well, I'm not pulling any extra weight down the river!" Rob said, a little too loudly to ignore. Suddenly, Heidi turned around in her seat and glared at us.

"Sorry to disappoint all of you," she said. "But I'm actually 133 pounds, and I'm not asexual. I've also rowed in an eight before, so I know exactly what all of you are supposed to be doing."

"And what is that?" Rob teased.

"Rowing together well and not carrying on like a bunch of grade-school boys who haven't reached puberty yet!"

"Hah-hah-hah!" Wean laughed. "Rob man, I think you just got nailed."

"Heidi, that was totally ballsy!" Porgy agreed. "Why don't you come and join us in the backseats!"

"Because there's no space," Heidi said.

"We'll make space," Porgy said.

"Yeah, you can sit on my lap," Wean offered.

"No thanks," Heidi said. "I prefer being up here in the first-class section."

Everyone laughed, and Heidi gave us a last glance over her shoulder, smiling with a triumphant look on her face. With her gray-blue eyes like a wise cat, I suspected that she had memorized every word that we had said and would use that information when the time was right.

CHAPTER TWELVE

Boys to Men

March is the cruelest month, but even more so for those who row.

While the rest of our classmates headed off to some Caribbean island to bronze their winter bodies in the sun, the sixty or so members of the Trinity Crew remained on campus for spring break and settled in to row double sessions. Naturally Coach Poole tried to sell us on the snake-oil notion that rowing twice a day was a total blast and definitely a much cooler thing to do than laze about on some random beach. After all, we would get super fit, he explained, and in exchange for a few weeks of physical hardship, we would then be treated to an evening of drama fit to rival Vaudeville—the infamous Trinity Crew Skit Night.

Head coach Norm Graf kicked off the first day of spring training with an impromptu pep talk to all of the squads, gathered in front of Bliss Boathouse. Graf had barely spoken to us freshmen before, but now that we had gotten through cuts, he apparently wanted to make a small gesture of group solidarity. He also wanted to take the opportunity to emphasize why it was important not to touch a drop of alcohol during the competitive season. All of the varsity athletes, it seemed, had heard this speech before, and most of them just stared at the ground, trying to keep a straight face as Graf launched into his annual sobriety pitch:

"Now all of you have been training quite hard, and when you do that, your body starts to build these extra blood vessels, in order to allow more oxygen to get from your lungs to your arms and legs . . ."

"Uh-oh," someone muttered. "It's Stormin' Norm's capillary speech . . ."

Graf glared at the interloper, silencing him.

"Now, there are the bigger blood vessels and veins that go in and out of the heart, and of course these get smaller and smaller as they move farther toward the extremities, branching out into tiny little capillaries and arterioles and so forth . . ."

He looked around to make sure everyone was paying attention to his lecture. He affected a professorial tone of voice now, as he continued to elaborate his scientific theory.

"The harder you train, the more capillaries you build, and this of course allows your body to transport oxygen more efficiently. But what happens if you should even take ONE sip of alcohol?"

He held out a long, bony finger and paused for a moment, waiting to see if any of us would dare reply.

"BOOM!" he yelled, clapping his big hands together. Some of the freshmen standing right beside him jumped back a bit and then laughed nervously.

"They explode like a pack of firecrackers! BOOM, BOOM, BOOM!" he cried, clapping thrice.

He paused again, lifting his bushy eyebrows for emphasis. I thought he seemed a little nutty, but I decided to keep my mouth shut. After all, I reckoned you had to be slightly crazed to coach crew for any length of time.

"Then all of that good work you've done has now been wasted, because you've killed them! You've murdered all of those poor little capillaries!" he explained.

We freshmen looked at each other, frowning in disbelief, and then back at Norm Graf. None of us really knew what to make of him, which was clearly the way he liked it.

"All right then, let's get on the water!" he concluded, abruptly shuffling off in his insulated pants and mad-bomber hat.

Sufficiently warned against the dangers of alcohol, we fetched our wooden boat, *The Connecticut*, off the rack and waited in line to put it into the water. It was named after the river we rowed on, and we had grown fond of it in the mildly obsessive way that all oarsmen become attached to their own equipment—including their oars and even the seats they sit upon. It was a George Pocock design, built especially for lightweight oarsmen, and many a good crew had rowed in it before us, including the women's varsity eight. The women were now rowing in one of the newer fiberglass shells made by Schoenbrod of Maine—not as pretty, I thought, but much stiffer and lighter.

As we waited in line, I briefly scanned the river. It was running high, with a strong current, and I knew that it would make rowing feel quite different in opposite directions. Heading downstream, our work would be light and easy, but rowing upstream was going to be a total slog, an enterprise only useful for building muscle. Then there were the cross currents that braided themselves under the footings of bridges, that could pitch a boat from side to side, like a cat playing with a mouse.

The wind had come up, too, and because of this, Heidi had us bring the boat down to our waists while we waited patiently for the final crews to launch. We were last in line because we were the frosh lights, the lowest crew on the totem pole. It was cold, and our fingers were already numb, even sheathed in the homemade pogies we'd fashioned from old wool socks. Even the coaches grumbled as they set up their aluminum skiffs, horsing the small outboards onto the transoms and then checking their gas tanks to make sure they were full enough. They didn't want to run out of gas on a day like today. Everything was made harder and slower in the cold, and both the coaches and the coxswains were dressed like lobstermen, insulated by down jackets and yellow rain pants. It was worse for them than it was for us, motoring about with no physical activity to keep their bodies warm.

Finally, we put *The Connecticut* into the gray-green water, tied in, and shoved off after a speedy countdown from bow. The current took us away almost immediately, and Heidi called upon the bow four to row us out of harm's way. There were numerous pilings to be avoided near the dock, as well as some seasonal flotsam and jetsam coursing through the stream, including half-submerged tree limbs that could easily puncture a wooden hull or at the very least strip off a rudder.

"STRONGER ON STARBOARD," Heidi called out.

"Bite me!" Wean replied from the bow.

"What did he say?" Heidi asked Pete Tyson.

"Oh, just ignore him," Tyson replied.

"Yo! No talking in the boat!" Dak boomed from the five seat. His deep voice carried more weight than anyone.

The boat fell silent as we made our way upstream, barely making headway in the strong current. Our new lineup was working well, with a few caveats. One was that Wean saw fit to mouth off from the hinterland of the bow seat, either to embarrass or impress Heidi. An experienced coxswain would have quickly told him to shut up, but she was still new to the job and didn't yet know how to deal with hostile backtalk. She wanted to please everyone, of course, at least at first. Most of us didn't really mind Wean's outbursts, which were mildly indecent and humorous in equal measure, but we felt sorry for Heidi, who was an overly tolerant soul.

The other challenge in our boat was that Pete Tyson, while being an excellent stroke, had a tendency to get excited and jack up the stroke rating whenever we started to race against the frosh heavies. I tried to settle him down whenever this happened, like a jockey with a thoroughbred horse, but he had little patience for the concept of ratio. It didn't help that Coach Poole had recently praised Peter to everyone as "the guy with the fastest legs in the boat," making our new stroke and the rest of us believe that leg speed was directly correlated to boat speed.

Collectively, those of us in the stern had also developed a slight attitude of superiority over our bow four counterparts, based on the ill-founded belief that we were somehow more relevant to the success of the boat. Peter's manic proclivities aside, we were smoother and longer drawing our blades through the water, while the bow four were short and punchy. I could feel the jerkiness of their strokes as they rowed us away from the dock, but I could also sense that they had undeniable power. Recently I had gotten into an impromptu wrestling match with Rob Leavitt, who was not much more than five feet six inches tall, and I was surprised to find that I could not move him. Porgy and Rhino were equally solid, and Wean, of course, was insanely strong, to match his overall personality.

Sensing our snobbish attitude, the bow four reveled in their outlier status, inciting moments of comic relief whenever possible. They often engaged in farting contests and constantly made fun of one another, bickering like a bunch of schoolchildren.

As Heidi brought in Dak and Henry Phillips, bringing us to sixes, the bow four launched into their daily banter.

"Robman, can you try to keep your blade in the water?" Wean quipped.

"OH . . . is *that* what I'm supposed to be doing?!" Rob shot back.

"Uh, yeah," Porgy chimed in.

"Shut up, butthead! How can you tell what my stroke looks like?"

"Because I have eyes in the back of my head," Porgy explained.

"That's funny," Rob said. "I've never seen a butt with eyes on it."

"Har! Har! Har!" Porgy barked, like a seal.

"Speaking of butts," he continued, "I think Rhino just farted."

"Did not!" said Rhino indignantly.

Peter and I could hear them up in the bow, carrying on like morons, but there was nothing we could do. Heidi needed to learn how to be more assertive. In the meantime, however, we had a larger problem on our hands. We'd been doing short race pieces with the heavyweights, and they had been beating us most of the time. On paper, heavyweights *should* be faster than lightweights, but we didn't know that—nor did we care. We just wanted to win. But as they came out on top more and more, Charlie began to spend more time with them. Naturally we began to equate their success with the lopsided amount of time he seemed to focus with the heavyweights.

"Look, Charlie is talking with the heavies again," Wean pointed out, as we began to row all eight now, completing our warm-up with some balance drills.

"Leave it alone," Dak boomed. "Don't say anything!"

And so, for the moment, everyone kept his mouth shut. But secretly Peter and I agreed that something had to be done. In the short run we decided that we were going to beat the heavies today, whatever the cost might be. We had barely gotten through our warm-up—a series of power tens and twenties—when the wind began to gust. It came out of the south and pushed hard against the flow of the current, creating rebellious, standing waves. A few of the larger ones broke over our bow.

"Shit!" Wean shouted. "I just got totally soaked!"

"OK, spin both boats!" Charlie called out through the megaphone, noticing the worsening conditions. "We'll do the first piece heading downstream."

As the two crews pivoted around and lined up, we eyed each other with gentle malice. We liked the heavies, but at the same time we wanted to kick their ass, and we were fairly certain that they felt the same way about us.

"Let's take them on this one!" Tyson whispered to Heidi.

I knew what that meant, and as we paddled forward and then took it up to full power, Peter brought the rate up to thirty-eight strokes a minute. We jumped ahead of the heavies a few seats, but it wasn't pretty. Our blades bounced off of random waves, and we struggled to keep the boat balanced.

"Take it down!" I said to Peter. But of course he was too excited to listen.

The heavies started to catch up, but we held them off. When we stopped rowing, everyone was happy.

"Yeah, baby!" Wean said, expressing the group sentiment.

"OK, spin again!" Charlie called out. "Next piece will be upstream."

"Now we're screwed," Rob pointed out. Against the current the heavies would have the clear advantage. With more mass their boat would juggernaut its way through the waves, whereas we would struggle just to make decent headway. We would have to try and overstroke them again, but this time it was going to be much more difficult.

The ports backed and the starboards rowed, and we had just gotten our boat turned around in the freshening breeze when Charlie called us into the second piece.

"Three to build!" he shouted.

Again, Peter tried to take up the rate, but this time it was a useless strategy. A few rollers came up over the stern decks and sloshed even more water into the boat. With all the deadweight in the hull, we were barely making headway.

"F—K!" Wean yelled.

"Keep rowing!" Dak bellowed.

"KEEP ROWING," Heidi echoed.

We were the farthest two crews away from the boathouse, and after we finished the piece, losing badly, we saw the heavies quickly spin their boat and begin to row back toward the dock as fast as they could. Either someone was sick, or something else was wrong. Charlie was with them, and he whipped his head around and called out:

"Head back—NOW!"

We tried to row, but the wind had gotten so strong now that it began to blow us sideways to the current, and straight toward a cluster of pilings that lay upstream of the dock. Several more waves swept over our gunnels in rapid succession, and suddenly our wooden hull was completely swamped.

"UNTIE! UNTIE!" Pete Tyson yelled. The icy water encircled our waists like a snake, squeezing the breath out of us.

"Stay with the boat!" Dak commanded. "Wait for Coach!"

But Charlie, of course, was with the heavyweights.

"Fuck that!" Wean said. The set of wooden pilings was now quite close, and he swam for them. The rest of the bow four followed his lead, abandoning ship.

By now the eight had rolled upside down in the current, making it harder to cling to the slippery cedar hull. Charlie motored up, flustered and worried.

"Get in!" he shouted. "Stern four first!"

We clambered into the launch, one at a time, and then Charlie revved forward to try and maneuver toward the bow four. Suddenly a gust of wind shoved his launch much faster forward than he intended.

"Damn!" he said. But it was too late.

His launch ran up and over our submerged eight, and we heard the prop begin to tear into the cedar skin hull. It made a sickening noise, like tree branches snapping. Finally he shifted into neutral and then dislodged himself from the eight by reversing direction. But now the current had taken him too quickly the other way—straight toward Rob Leavitt, clinging to the pilings.

"Watch out!" Rob cried, holding out one arm. The half-submerged engine came grinding toward him, with the prop spinning wildly in reverse. It was inches from his legs, and Rob had to straight-arm the small outboard to hold it at bay. Charlie finally reversed direction and moved away.

"I can't take you guys!" he shouted to the bow four. "Stay here and I'll come back."

As we left the bow four clinging to the pilings, I immediately felt a new sense of respect for Wean, Porgy, Rob, and Rhino, for none of them was complaining now. Wean, in fact, had managed to shimmy up one of the poles like a monkey, and he soon had the other three laughing at his antics, taking their minds off their precarious situation. Fortunately another coach soon came by and collected them before hypothermia set in.

Back at the dock, we stripped off most of our wet clothes, and the coxswains began to scurry about doing head counts. Ours wasn't the only crew that had swamped that day, but our boat was the sole casualty in terms of damage. As Charlie towed it back to the dock, we were still in a mild state of shock, wondering what had happened to it. We took the oars out of the oarlocks and then drained the water out of the inside of the hull by alternately tilting and lifting it. It was only after we hauled it back to the boathouse on our shoulders and put it in slings that we saw the huge holes, like shark bites in the side of a whale.

"Get back to campus and get warm," Charlie said. "I'll deal with this."

No one said a word. We all knew it was destroyed.

"Rob man, are you OK?" Heidi asked as we walked toward the van. Rob nodded.

"Wean man?"

"Yeah . . ."

"Porgy man?"

Heidi went down the whole boat, making sure everyone was OK. We were all present, but we were not all right. We had lost our boat for the remainder of the season and didn't know if there was anything to replace it. Something else had changed, too, although we could not talk about it. Riding back to campus in the post-row silence, I felt like any dissension existing within the crew had all been washed away in the day's calamity. We had survived a cruel baptism in the Connecticut River, and we knew we were lucky to be alive.

Chapter Thirteen

Dress Rehearsal

Sometimes there is only one remedy for tragedy, and that is comedy.

Naturally it was none other than Jeff Jowurski (aka Mongo) who took it upon himself to rescue us from the cycle of despair that could have sucked us downward into the cesspool of self-pity. At dinner that night he acted as if the tragic events of the day were no big deal—they were, in fact, rather heroic and fun. After all, he and the varsity heavyweight squad had also swamped, and one of their guys, Barr Flynn, had barely made it back to the boathouse alive. Another had swum all the way back to shore. Mongo admitted that we frosh lights had experienced a harrowing ordeal, but explained that the JV lights had also managed to break off their bow and only stayed afloat because their coach smartly wedged his jacket into the gaping hole. All in all, it had been a banner day, at least in Mongo's mind.

Being a mathematics major, he even came up with the following binary equivalence relation: Death-defying = Life-enhancing.

Just in case we didn't hear him talking loudly, he began to catapult corn bread and chocolate pudding at us using his spoon. The corn bread gave more heft to the mixture, allowing it greater range, and the pudding made it stain-worthy. When he got bored of this juvenile behavior, he stood up on his chair to make a big announcement. He looked like King Kong, only with glasses.

"OK, everyone, listen up! It's time to figure out Skit Night," he announced. "All freshmen report to the basement of Sever Hall in one hour. No exceptions!"

Everyone groaned, except for Sam Bradshaw, the captain of the frosh heavies. Bradshaw loved anything to do with crew and probably would have stuck his head in a toilet bowl if Mongo had suggested it. The rest of us were completely exhausted from the afternoon, however, and the last thing we wanted to do was deal with Jowurski, who had obviously elected himself as theatrical director for this thespian debacle. Naturally, though, we didn't have a choice. So after we'd sponged the chocolate pudding off of our splash jackets, the ten women and seventeen men who composed the freshman squads dragged our tired bodies over to Sever Hall after dinner. The girls, at least, had taken showers; most of the guys hadn't even bothered.

"All right, all right," Mongo said, when we were all assembled. "I've got a lot of great ideas here, so shut up and listen!"

He pulled a dirty napkin out of his pocket and squinted at some notes he had scribbled down. Carl Rox, the varsity heavy cocaptain, was also helping out. Carl looked about thirty years old and had a permanent dumbass smile on his face that was barely concealed by a heavily manicured mustache. He just stood there, trying to look burly, smirking at us with his arms crossed while he scoped out the freshman women.

"The first skit will be a reenactment of the sinking of *The Connecticut*, using this scale model that Carl has created," Mongo explained.

On cue, Carl produced a long baguette that he'd pilfered from the dining hall and placed it on the table in front of us. It was supposed to resemble our boat. He'd also fashioned little clay figures to represent oarsmen, and he placed these on top of the French bread after he'd sliced it in half and dug out some of the innards. Finally he stuck plastic spoons into the sides of the baguette to serve as oars. You could tell that he was pretty impressed with his workmanship. We were all so tired that we just watched him put together this absurd-looking model, wondering what would come next.

"OK, this will be like the 'Mr. Bill' show on *Saturday Night Live*," Carl explained. He had a flat, matter-of-fact voice, like an attorney who was about to demonstrate how an accident happened, using ridiculous scale-model props.

Mr. Bill was a clay figurine that nearly always got crushed or disfigured in some tragic incident, usually at the hands of his nemesis, Mr. Sluggo. Luckily, since Mr. Bill was made out of clay, he was always reborn for the next episode, only to experience another terrible tragedy. Mr. Bill also had a weird, high-pitched voice and always cried out, "OH NOOOOO!" whenever something bad happened.

Carl proceeded to demonstrate the basic narrative. Coach Poole, renamed Coach Sluggo, drove around in a launch fashioned from a Dairy Queen chili dog container. He ran over our baguette boat repeatedly, crushing a few of the clay figures that represented members of the crew. We were all, essentially, Mr. Bill. I had to admit it was pretty funny, in an over-the-top sort of way, especially when Carl Rox broke into a falsetto voice as our French baguette boat got run over. He tore a few more pieces out of the loaf and ate them as the skit proceeded.

"OH NOOOOO!" he cried, with his mouth full of French bread.

"All right, all right," Mongo cut in. "Not bad. But now *I've* got an idea. We just need someone to play Hose . . ."

He scanned the room for volunteers, but no one stepped forward.

Hose was the nickname of Andy Sanders, a former Trinity coxswain who had graduated a few years back and was now coaching the women's team. None of us knew the origins of his nickname, but Mongo was about to reveal all.

"Get over here, Boyne," he said.

"What?" I said. "Why me?"

"'Cause I said so," he barked. "Besides you're tall and scrawny like Andy. Here—take this."

He handed me a giant-size super-soaker squirt gun.

"What am I supposed to do with that?" I said.

"What do you think, moron? You're going to walk on stage with it and hose down the entire audience, including all the coaches."

"But I'll get killed afterward," I protested.

"Not my problem," Mongo said. "Now remember to wait until I give you the cue: HEY ANDY, HOW COME THEY CALL YOU HOSE? And tuck this thing down the back of your pants, like a gangster, so people won't know what's coming."

He spun me around and put the gun in place.

"Now go and rehearse," he said, kicking me in the backside.

There was no need for me to practice the dumb skit, of course, but I did take the opportunity to distance myself from Mongo and Carl in order to avoid getting chosen for the next act. That one was even more outrageous, because eleven volunteers would be required to moon the audience. The bow four of our boat readily volunteered, of course, as well as Sam Bradshaw and a few of the braver members of the women's team who didn't mind displaying their derrieres.

"OK," Mongo said, "This is going to be the grand finale. All of you guys and gals will have to write one letter on your butt that will collectively spell out S-P-R-I-N-G B-R-E-A-K. Then, on my cue, you'll form a chorus line and drop your pants. Understood?"

Everyone nodded, and Wean grinned with delight.

"But how do we write a letter on our own butts?" Porgy asked.

"Figure that out yourself, Einstein," Mongo said, handing him a blue Sharpie.

"OK, practice up! See you in ten days."

As we turned our backs to leave, Mongo and Carl Rox kicked us in the backsides again with their boots. It was the closest thing to affection they could muster.

"Jeez, those guys are a couple of knuckleheads," Rhino said.

We went back to our dorms, slightly unnerved but in much better spirits.

Tomorrow simply had to be a better day.

Luckily my basketball-playing roommate was away at a tournament, so I got ready to settle in for a good night's sleep. Just before I dozed off, however, there was an urgent-sounding knock on my door.

"Yeah. Who is it?" I said.

"It's Porgy. Open up!"

"Jesus, it's nearly midnight. What do you want?"

I opened my door a crack, suspicious.

"Boyne man, can you write the letter K on my ass."

"What?" I said. "Are you drunk?"

"Well . . . Rob man and I might've had a few beers," Porgy admitted. "But it was totally necessary after today's ordeal."

"OK, fine," I said, finally letting him in. "But Skit Night isn't for another ten days. Why the big rush?"

"Because if I wait, I might forget," he said. "Plus, I may as well get it over with, so I don't have to worry about it anymore."

I looked at him blankly. Then I looked down the hallway in both directions to see if this was some sort of prank, but no one was there.

"OK, hurry up. Drop your pants," I said, suddenly feeling sympathy for doctors.

I quickly took the Sharpie and tattooed his butt with the letter K. It's actually harder than you might think to draw straight lines on someone's backside, by the way, which is much like cross-country skiing over hill and dale. Of course, just as I was finishing up, Heidi, who lived only a few rooms away, opened her door and witnessed Porgy pulling up his gray sweatpants.

"Well, hell—o!" she said, lifting her eyebrows and smiling.

"Wait. It's not what you think," I said.

"Hey, I'm totally cool with that sort of thing," Heidi said, and then wandered downstairs to the Jarvis bathrooms to brush her teeth.

"That's just great, Porgy," I said. "Now look what you've done!"

Porgy just laughed, in his drunken stupor. "Aw, that's nothing. She was probably just checking out my awesome ass!"

"Uh, yeah, I'm sure that was it. Now can I please get some sleep?" I said, pushing him out of my doorway.

"OK, OK!" he said. "Take it easy . . . now wait a sec. Are you sure you did a good job? I mean, do you have a mirror so I can check it out?"

"No, I don't have a freaking mirror! Now get lost!"

Porgy reluctantly tightened the drawstring of his gray sweatpants and trundled off like a badger, still nervous about his upcoming performance. Heidi had just come back upstairs, and he waved to her and said good night. She passed by my door as I was still standing there.

"I can explain . . ." I said.

"Mum's the word," she smiled and winked, pretending to lock her lips with an invisible key. I just shook my head and closed my door.

When I finally got to sleep, after resigning myself to the absurdity of the evening, I was haunted by a host of bizarre scenes that rivaled the skits Mongo and Carl had produced. In the last dream series of the night, our lightweight crew was in the last five hundred meters of a two thousand–meter race, locked in battle with an unnamed opponent. The faces of the other oarsmen were shadowy, but I could almost make them out in the periphery of my vision. Every time I tried to gaze directly over at them, however, they disappeared like ghosts. I knew they were still there, because their cox'n kept hammering away at the gunnels of their boat with the knobs of the rudder cables—*Tock! Tock! Tock!* The guys in my crew worked harder and harder to break free, but I began to sense that our efforts were futile. There was something creepy about this other crew that clung to us, like a dark shadow.

CHAPTER FOURTEEN

The Ghost Boat

I woke up feverish and sweaty, exhausted from the nightmare of the imagined crew race.

Suddenly I heard the knocking from my dream again, and for a moment I thought I'd finally lost my mind. Double sessions had already gotten to me, and we were only a few days in. I drew in a long breath and let it out slowly. Then I realized that the knocking was actually coming from my door.

"Hey, get out of bed, butthead! We'll be late for practice," said a familiar voice. It was Rob Leavitt, the three seat of our boat. He'd been banging away for several minutes, trying to wake me up.

"Ugh," I responded. I reached for a bottle of aspirin and popped four into my mouth. Without water, they went down like small rocks. Then I threw on my damp rowing clothes from the day before, still drying on the radiator, and joined Rob in the hallway.

"You look like crap," he said.

"Thanks," I told him. "Your breath smells like crap."

"I guess that makes us even," he replied. Rob was premed and had a very pragmatic view on everything.

"Yep."

"Double sessions suck," Rob offered, as we slid into his yellow VW Beetle, which I'd nicknamed the Yellow Submarine. He often drove me to practice, since we lived pretty close to each other in the main quad.

"Yep."

"Not much of a conversationalist this morning," he observed.

"Nope."

Rob drove like a New York City taxi driver, but he was quite skilled at finding the best back roads through East Hartford. Despite our late start, we arrived nearly on time and wandered into the musty bays, barely lit by a few ceiling fluorescents, and joined the rest of the team. Everyone was gathered around a new boat that Charlie had just finished rigging, sitting right-side up in a pair of slings. Heidi was inspecting the stern cables, and Joe was running his hand along the smooth white hull. It was a fiberglass Schoenbrod that the junior varsity heavyweights weren't using this season, she explained, since they'd been reduced to a four-oared shell due to injuries.

"So it's a freakin' heavyweight hand-me-down," Wean said in disgust.

"Yeah, but it's pretty new—I don't think it even has a name yet," Heidi speculated.

"It's the great white whale!" Rob said, drawing a few laughs.

"No, it's Casper the Friendly Ghost!" Henry Phillips offered. Everyone looked at him in silence and frowned at the missed attempt at humor.

"Who is Casper the Friendly Ghost?" Porgy asked, frowning.

"Never mind," Henry said.

Porgy looked over at me for help, but when our eyes met, they quickly fell away, suddenly remembering our tattoo-parlor antics from the previous night.

"My shoes are too big," he said, trying to change the subject.

"Now let's not make too many prejudgments," Dak advised. "The boat is known as *The Gray*, I believe."

"Well, whatever it's called, it looks cool to me," Joe said, running his hand over the hull again. "Smooth as a baby's bottom."

"Jeez, Joe. You're from the Planet Weird. You know that, right?" Wean said.

"I am not," Joe replied. "I'm from California."

Everyone laughed. "Same thing," Wean said.

"All right, take the oars down!" Heidi bellowed, calling the practice to order.

Whatever the name of the boat might be, it was ours.

As soon as we put the new shell in the water and tied in, we realized that things were going to be different. Many coaches will try to convince you that it is the people in the crew that are of primary importance, and not the boat itself. Boat manufacturers, of course, will tell you the very opposite, that a good boat can make all the difference in the world. The reality, of course, lies somewhere in between. A crew must certainly believe in their boat and trust that it will carry them forward to their best effort. But as we were about to discover, it goes much further beyond that simple truth. For like a horse and a rider, there exists a dynamic relationship between a crew and their boat that can profoundly influence success.

Our new eight was certainly oversize, but on the plus side, it was noticeably lighter in weight, making it easier to carry and move through the water. We noticed this immediately as we started paddling, along with how tricky it was to balance. With our boat average of 149 pounds per man, there was barely any displacement of the hull in the water. On the other hand, our overbuoyant boat was much more responsive to everything we did, which forced us to row better as we progressed through our ritual warm-up drills.

Coach Poole followed along behind us in his launch, watching how we adjusted to the Schoenbrod and seeing if we could handle the bigger hull. The answer came soon, just after we'd finished our warm-up drills and Heidi called out, "Weigh enough!" After the final stroke, we feathered our blades out of the water in perfect unison and the hull magically found its precise centerline. None of our blades touched the water, and Heidi had us hold the pause and balance as long as we could, until the boat came to an eerie standstill.

Everyone was silent. Charlie cut his engine, watching in disbelief.

"Let fall!" Heidi finally said with delight in her voice. We slapped our blades down to the water in unison.

"Balls. Balls. Balls. Seeds. Seeds. Seeds. Cubes. Cubes. Cubes!" Wean concluded.

Charlie beamed.

"OK, I wasn't going to have you guys do any pieces today, but let's try a few five hundreds with the heavies just to see what happens at full pressure," he said.

We paddled up alongside the heavies, who were still in a wooden shell, *The Hartford*, and then Coach Poole called out "Three to build!"

Peter Tyson brought us up to a solid thirty-two, then thirty-four, strokes a minute, and as we found our rhythm, something magical happened. Stroke followed stroke in flawless succession, and suddenly it felt like we were barely working. We were flying. The fiberglass hull, which was now barely touching the water, started making a very particular and pleasing sound, like a cat that begins to purr when it is scratched just right. The hull gurgled as the trickle of water flowed beneath it, like the sound of a hidden, underground spring.

We flew by the heavies and beat them by a boat length. Then we did it again, and again. Seven times. They were so caught off guard, they didn't know what to say. After all, lightweights weren't supposed to beat heavyweights, especially not in a heavyweight hull. No one in our crew said a word either, for what had just happened defied logic. We were the wrong size for the boat, and it was tippy at rest, but somehow it sprouted wings when we all started rowing together at the right speed.

All we had to do was find "the gurgle."

Our spirits still high, we returned to Bliss Boathouse and put the boat back on the rack, wiping it down with care.

"Pegasus," Joe said. "I think we should call it Pegasus."

"You're weird, Joe," Wean said.

"No, seriously. It's a magical boat," Joe said.

"OK, our first race is in less than two weeks!" Charlie announced, when both crews were assembled. "The Coast Guard Academy in New London, Connecticut."

I felt my heart lift up into my throat, where it would take up permanent residency for the next several days.

CHAPTER FIFTEEN

Close Call at Coast Guard

It was our first race of the spring season, and for many of us it was our first real regatta. The Head of the Charles hadn't really counted, for despite all of its history and spectator appeal, that chaotic obstacle course was simply a race against the clock that just happened to have other crews in it. By contrast, the spring regattas, with their side-by-side format, offered an intensity and conclusiveness more akin to a boxing match, where victory was less open to debate. To me, the pugilistic metaphor was even more appropriate: Trinity might be going head-to-head with Coast Guard, its archrival, but I was going toe-to-toe with Samuel Caluso, the bully who had made my life miserable back in high school.

"So what did this guy do to you again?" Dak asked. He and I were sitting together on the bus ride south, toward New London and Long Island Sound.

"He basically tortured me," I mumbled. "He saw himself as a much better athlete, because I ran cross-country and he played football."

"But now you're an oarsman," Dak said, grinning.

"Yeah. And so is he."

"Well, we'll see about that!" Dak said.

Dak was the most reserved, humble guy on the frosh light squad, and he was our stalwart captain. In part this was because of his prior rowing experience at Exeter, a New England prep school known for producing excellent oarsmen, but also it was due to Dak's calm demeanor and evenhanded, intelligent opinion on almost any subject. He had a deep, basso voice that made you believe every word that came out of his mouth.

"I'm going to let you in on a little secret," he said, lowering his voice. "When I was a senior at Exeter, I was quite a bit heavier than I am now and not in very good shape. Not one of my old teammates would recognize me now or believe that I could ever make it as a lightweight. Anyway, back then, I lost a seat race to a guy who was much bigger and better than me, and it was totally embarrassing."

"What was the other guy's name?" I asked.

"Jon Smith," he said.

"And where is he now?"

"He rows heavyweight crew at Brown."

"Well, now you're a Trinity lightweight!" I said.

"We'll see about that, too," Dak said. "After all, we still have to weigh in!"

We both laughed. With his deep voice and measured way of speaking, Dak had a way of instantly making you feel better.

—⁓—

Just three days before, he had come to my dorm room and coaxed me out of a forty-eight-hour delirium. Halfway through spring break, I'd picked up an intense flu that quickly burned through my body and left me with no strength. For days afterward I felt so leaden I couldn't even drag myself over to health services. Then Dak appeared, bearing a cup of hot chicken soup from the dining hall.

"How are you feeling?" he asked.

"Not great," I croaked, my voice scratchy and my brain abuzz with fever.

"So I gather. But here's the thing. We've got Coast Guard coming up in a few days, and we can't race without you. The new boat sucks without our old seven seat—we can't even seem to set it up!"

"Who is subbing in for me?" I asked, sitting up and taking a sip of the soup.

"Charlie actually sat in once. But mostly Bill Windridge from the JV lights."

"Oh no," I said.

"Oh yeah," Dak said. "It's really bad. And Windridge talks all the time . . ."

"OK," I said. "I'll be there tomorrow—rain or shine."

The next day I took a handful of aspirin and forced myself up. I felt oddly disconnected from my body, as if I were wearing a snowsuit saturated with water. I could feel my heart thumping in my chest, just from the effort of walking to the car. I was still weak, but I didn't let on.

As soon as I got in the boat and started rowing again, however, my spirits instantly lifted and my senses came alert and clarified in the open air. I didn't have much strength, but as I fell into rhythm with the rest of the crew, I slowly felt my body begin to regenerate, like a car with a dead battery getting a jump start. And when the Schoenbrod began to make its familiar gurgling noise, everyone knew that we had our mojo back.

Heidi called out, "Weigh enough," and when we feathered our blades out of the water, the boat set up like a rock. It ran out, perfectly balanced, for a full minute, just as it had the first time we had rowed in it. Charlie had been following us once again, just to make sure I was going to be OK.

"Welcome back, Dan," he said. "I guess the boat likes you!"

"Yeah, Bill Windridge sucked!" Wean said.

Everyone laughed. That was about as good as it got in terms of brotherly love from the guys on the team. After all, we had a job to do, and there was no time to be wasted on the trivialities of affection.

—～—

As we headed south, toward Long Island Sound, I was returning to the little shoreline towns of my childhood—Old Saybrook, Guilford, Branford, Westbrook. Our bus banked a left onto coastal I-95, crossing over the broad mouth of the Connecticut River and then the Thames, traversing the same route that my sister and I had once taken on our way to daily sculling lessons at Blood Street Sculls. Not far beyond lay the Mystic River and Mystic Seaport, where we'd gone to sailing camp as kids. As the sea air wafted in through the open windows of our bus, some of these memories returned to me. There was something magical about the ocean, and just the smell of it began to get me excited. To be out on the sea, in a boat of any sort, always promised an adventure, although today our trip was directed toward a single purpose.

We were certainly going to the appropriate place for a waterborne battle. Both the Groton naval sub base and the Coast Guard Academy were tucked away just inside the mouth of the Thames, flanking each other on either side of the river. I spotted one of the Coast Guard gunboats as we went over the Gold Star Bridge, as well as a classic training vessel called *The Eagle*. Both were painted white with a trademark red and blue stripe running diagonally down the bow. They looked grand. By now everyone else was peering out the window, starting to get excited for our first spring race.

In the rowing world, the Thames was known to many as the site of the Harvard-Yale Regatta, the oldest intercollegiate competition in the country. Nobody in our freshman crew really knew or cared about that race, though, for it was an exclusive rivalry that didn't include us, or for that matter the local crews who plied the Thames every day, including Coast Guard and Connecticut College. To them these two Ivy League schools were merely summer tourists who came and went, occupying their prime river real estate, or "camps," for only a week or so. As we pulled into Coast Guard, the austere-looking gated campus certainly didn't evoke a relaxed summer camp atmosphere. We quickly spotted some cadets in full dress uniform, drilling in formation on the playing fields. It was a bit intimidating to those of us from the laid-back liberal arts campus at Trinity, and we suspected that the rules here were different.

As soon as we got off the bus, we felt the bite of the sea breeze coming off the water. Charlie walked over toward the river to check out the conditions and to shake hands with head coach Bill Stowe. The Thames was a much wider swath of water than we were used to back in Hartford, and bearings would have to be taken from buoys more so than trees or other landmarks. Heidi marched off to the coxswains' meeting to get the exact details, while the rest of us wandered over toward the boathouse to weigh in.

Packed inside the small locker room like a bunch of cattle, the lightweight teams stood around and waited for their turn to get weighed. There were some old Head of the Charles rowing posters on the wall, and the peppermint scent of tiger balm liniment and the must of dirty laundry intermingled in the room, creating a nauseating effect.

"157 . . . 142 . . . 141 . . . 159.5 . . . 155 . . . 139 . . . 145 . . . 152," an official called out as the Trinity frosh lights stepped on and off the scale.

Then it was Coast Guard's turn.

"158 . . . 151 . . . 155 . . . 157 . . . 154 . . . 156 . . . 152 . . . 156."

Coast Guard outweighed us by more than five pounds per man.

Like Dak, I knew that Sam Caluso had been huskier during his high school days, but as I caught my first glimpse of him, stepping onto the scale, I noticed that we were now remarkably similar in build. As I took in his full measure, it suddenly struck me as odd that two people so disparate in physical strength and size could somehow, in such a short period of time, come to almost resemble one another. The main difference between us now was that he had a crew cut and I had long hair.

After weigh-in, I noticed him chatting with his boat mates, nodding over toward me and chuckling, then slapping them on the back. I imagined him saying something like, "Look at those Trinity wimps—this race is going to be a cinch." But somehow I wasn't afraid of him anymore. I had my teammates around me now, and I knew that our crew was good. Being a member of a rowing team was a completely different experience than being on a running team, especially when it came to competitions. Runners were individualists at heart, while rowers stuck close together and acted more like members of a gang—after all, they completely relied on one another.

Charlie had told us to be polite but not chatty until after the race, so we all kept our distance from the other team. We were representing Trinity College now, and it was expected that our performance would be exemplary on all fronts—especially at Coast Guard. Norm Graf, who had attended the Culver Military Academy in his youth, was a stickler for obeying protocol. So we dutifully went back outside after the weigh-in and began to rig our boat on the grassy playing fields, now devoid of drilling cadets. I noticed that Caluso's crew had a Schoenbrod racing shell, just like ours, set up with the standard port stroke configuration. Maybe our mysterious bucket rig would intimidate Coast Guard, I mused. I could see them eyeing us, too, as the prerace tension mounted.

"Hey," Dak said, "Check it out. I think your buddy is rowing number seven, just like you."

"That's crazy," I said. "I mean, that's impossible!"

But as Coast Guard shouldered their boat and headed off the dock, I saw that Dak was right. Caluso was standing opposite the seven-seat rigger.

Suddenly I was nervous again.

Athletes exhibit a variety of odd behaviors before competitions, and oarsmen are no exception to the rule. Some play loud music, seeking to drown out their nerves, while others go off and sit quietly, trying to visualize their ultimate performance. On our freshman lightweight team, only Joe Rhineman seemed to be capable of the latter—I spotted him seated in a cross-legged yoga position under the shell trailer—while the rest of us engaged in more juvenile exhibitions of prerace jitters. Wean started chattering like an angry squirrel, then climbed the shell trailer as if it were a jungle gym. Porgy and Rob began to wrestle with one another. All of us took turns dashing off to the porta potty every few minutes, knowing that soon we would be on the water.

Thankfully Heidi soon called for "hands on" before anyone got hurt. And from that moment on, everything became very focused. Drugged with adrenaline, we now relied on her commands and our prerowing rituals to guide us.

"TIE IN! COUNT DOWN FROM BOW WHEN READY! SHOVE OFF IN TWO—ONE! TWO!"

We were off, rowing in fours, then sixes, doing our pic drills as flawlessly as possible as we paraded away from the dock. Much later on in my rowing career, I would observe crews as they warmed up like this, and come to the conclusion that how they executed these simple preliminaries could often predict their success or failure. Our frosh light crew had excellent technique, or so Charlie had told us. But did we have enough power? I felt like my energy level was only at 75 percent, coming off my week of illness. How strong was Caluso and his crew of cadets? *Focus on your own boat*, I repeated to myself, echoing a phrase that Charlie had told us. Before we left, he explained that the race might be decided in the last five hundred meters, where the course was less protected from the wind. There the water would get rough and truly test the mettle of each crew, when we were tired and grinding out the final strokes toward the finish line.

"Remember, some races are decided by a single stroke," he said. "Focus on each one and make all of them count."

His words turned out to be prophetic. The Thames River had become quite choppy and full of strong current as we finished our prerace warm-up and then slowly backed our way into one of the two anchored launches that served as starting platforms, or "stake boats." A volunteer from Coast Guard grabbed on to our stern and tried to hold it fast as the wind continued to bat us about, threatening to swing us sideways, straight into our opponents, who were setting themselves up in the next launch over.

Both crews went off the line hard and fast, at a forty-two, and settled down to a reasonable thirty-three strokes per minute.

"We have two seats!" Heidi shouted. "Let's take two more."

Peter pushed the stroke rate up two beats, to a thirty-five, and we edged forward. But Coast Guard hung on and then started to advance, gaining back some of what they'd lost. By one thousand meters, we still held on to a small lead, but then our boat started slowly veering away from our opponents, as if Heidi were heading toward the wrong finish line.

"HARDER ON STARBOARD!" she shouted, trying to get us back on course. The Schoenbrod responded, but it wasn't pretty, and you could feel the boat pitching down to port, due to the unevenness of pressure on the two sides.

Because our boat had strayed from its original lane, it was now hard to tell who had the advantage. Both crews now entered the last five hundred, where the water became choppier.

"SPRINT!" I heard the Coast Guard coxswain shout. Their boat immediately starting moving on us, and some of their guys were shouting now—urging each other to make one last push. We were already at a thirty-eight and couldn't seem to bring it up any higher. Our starboards were still working overtime to keep us on course, and I felt myself just trying to hold the boat together, translating Peter's overaggressive stroke rating to a group of guys behind me who were struggling to keep their rhythm.

Then suddenly Coast Guard faded, dropping back a full length. Out of the corner of my eye, I saw that one of their guys had crabbed just twenty strokes from the finish line. It wasn't a boat stopper, but by the time they found their rhythm again, we had cruised across the finish line, a boat length and bit of open water ahead. We abruptly stopped rowing after we crossed the line and caught our breath. Peter pumped his fist in the air and a few other guys in the stern cheered, but in the bow of the boat there were multiple shouts of confusion.

"What the hell happened with the steering?" Wean demanded. He was super pissed off, because the starboards had needed to pull extra hard during the second half of the race.

"I don't know," Heidi said. "It must have been the current or something."

"We could have lost!" Rob said. "If they hadn't crabbed—"

"But we didn't," Dak said. "So leave it alone."

Everyone finally calmed down. Postrace emotions, it seemed, could run as high as prerace jitters. We paddled back to the dock in silence, took our boat out of the water, and set it in slings. Soon the mystery of the bad steering was revealed, when Charlie discovered a loose rudder cable, which made moving our boat to port nearly impossible without the extra power of the starboard oarsmen. Heidi was exonerated and Wean and Rob were pacified, leaving the rest of us free to enjoy our win.

After our boat was derigged and put away, we waited for the sweet moment when our opponents would have to give us their shirts. It was one of the best rituals of spring rowing, supposedly started by Harvard and Yale, not far from where we were all standing. Originally the transfer of shirts happened on the water, and one crew would have to row back to the dock shirtless. But even on dry land, the betting shirt ritual was like a ritual scalping. And for me it was a nearly inconceivable moment, as I watched Caluso and his crew slowly advance toward us, holding their betting shirts in hand. I could tell they were pretty upset, for all of the other Coast Guard crews had beaten Trinity that day. They were the only losers.

"Good race," I said, extending my hand.

"Yeah—one of our guys caught a crab," Caluso quickly replied, avoiding my handshake by handing me his shirt, which he'd bundled up into a messy ball.

"We had issues with our steering cables," I countered.

He nodded, taking in this new information. There was an awkward moment of silence. Both of us had played our trump cards, and now neither one of us knew what to say. Our past history hung in the air between us like old refuse.

"How's Trinity?" he finally asked.

"Great," I said. "How's Coast Guard?"

Caluso shrugged. "It's OK. If you join the crew team, you get extra off-campus privileges," he volunteered, and then admitted that almost every minute of his day was scheduled.

"Oh," I said, "that must suck."

He shrugged again. Another awkward silence followed.

"OK, well, we'll meet you again at the Nationals," he said. "I suppose then we'll really see who has the better crew."

"Yep. See you then," I said, flat of affect.

After Caluso walked away, I quickly opened up my prize to admire it. That's when I noticed all the dirty boat grease smeared into the white fabric.

"Nice shirt," Dak said, leaning over my shoulder.

"Thanks," I said. I glanced at his betting shirt, and it was spotless.

"Don't worry, that crud should wash off with a little detergent," he said.

"I hope so," I said, looking down at the grimy shirt.

"Hey," Dak said. "Lighten up. The main thing is that you beat him, right? And we just won our first race!"

"Yeah," I said. "You're absolutely right."

I gave him a high five, and then we collected our gear and walked back to the bus. We were moving slower now, as the adrenaline of the race began to wear off. Soon exhaustion set in, and my legs became leaden. My lungs felt like I'd just smoked a pack of cigarettes.

"Still feeling sick?" Dak asked.

I shook my head. "I'm OK, but I still don't feel great about the race."

"Why?"

"I don't know," I admitted, after we'd boarded the bus. "Somehow it didn't feel clean—I mean with that Coast Guard guy catching a crab and all."

"Hey, that's part of racing," Dak said. "Remember what Charlie said—every stroke counts."

I nodded, then leaned over against the bus window to rest.

But during the ride back to Hartford, after everyone had fallen into a postrace slumber, I was still awake. My mind kept replaying the race over again, and then the awkward exchange with Caluso afterward. *Then we'll really see who has the better crew*, he had said. Those words stung me like a bee, and deep in my brain I knew that he was right. I'd have to face him and his Coast Guard crew again, to erase any doubt as to which crew was the best.

CHAPTER SIXTEEN

The Stern Pair

In crew you often become closest to the guys you sit immediately beside, and Peter Tyson and I were no exception. As the stern pair, we were often in dialogue about various rowing and non-rowing matters, with Peter usually proposing the more direct path toward the endgame. I was more circumspect and always brought into consideration the means by which one got there. Despite our differences, Peter and I generally got along well—except when it came to the question of stroke ratings. In my opinion anything over a thirty-six was pure lunacy and unsustainable over two thousand meters. For Peter, crew racing was a spontaneous exercise and setting limits was a big mistake. We hadn't yet come to terms on this point, and our next race was coming up soon.

Occasionally the two of us made excursions around campus, and one night Peter showed up at my door and proposed that we climb the Trinity Chapel, which afforded a spectacular view of Hartford and beyond.

"But isn't that illegal?" I objected.

"Sure, but you just sneak around the back," he said.

"How do you get to the top?" I asked. "Are there stairs?"

"Of course not. You have to scale the outside."

Naturally, in the end, Peter scuttled all of my objections and we stole out across the quad under the darkness of a new moon. It was springtime at last, and the smell of fresh-cut grass hung in the air, inspiring us to do something a bit more daring than simply playing Frisbee on the quad. The Trinity Chapel was the architectural centerpiece on campus, and while the student population was no longer solely Episcopal, the stone edifice still had an undeniable presence, with its elegant cloisters and curious, figure-laden archways. Carillon music issued from the upper reaches of its bell tower at random hours, and below, many important campus rituals like freshman convocation still took place within its walls.

Most people who attend schools like Trinity have forgotten that one of the original purposes of a liberal arts college was to impart a broad-based education directed toward a greater appreciation of the divine. The theory, in fact, was pretty simple—for if God indeed knew all things, then an exposure to the full spectrum of worldly knowledge could move students a bit closer to that sense of omniscient being. Nowadays, however, the idea seems to have lost merit, as many undergraduates are herded toward math, computer science, or business fields of study.

Whether rowing was a part of this original liberal arts plan, or simply a British import adopted from the days of muscular Christianity, where athletics were also proposed as a method to produce well-rounded, moral men capable of self-sacrifice and teamwork, is hard to say. Peter and I thought very little about these matters as we snuck around to the back of the church, dodging the floodlights that illuminated its outer walls.

Luckily the campus security guards had better things to do that night than patrol the outskirts of the chapel. We really didn't want to be spotted, however, so we waited until the coast was clear. Then we made our move. With Peter it was always a simple "follow me" style of play. He would rush forward quickly into whatever activity he was doing, daring others to participate. This unguarded enthusiasm was generally rewarded, and it was only afterward that the potential dangers of the enterprise were revealed.

The first stretch of our ascent involved holding on to a woven steel cable that normally served as a ground wire for the church in the event of lightning storms. Peter grabbed the cable, leaned back, and propped his feet up into the corner crevice of the building. Then he began to scale the back corner of the main church wall, disappearing into the darkness.

When he made it to the top he called out, "Your turn!"

The thirty-foot free climb was no cakewalk. I had to lay back quite a bit to maintain enough leg pressure against the wall, and the awkward position was not for the fainthearted. This sort of climbing, I mused, was a lot like rowing. In both cases you simply held on for dear life, hauling away with your arms, while you kept furiously pumping with your legs. The consequences of letting go or giving up were not worth dwelling on.

Luckily the chill of the night air and a shot of adrenaline gave me just the extra boost I needed. When I safely ascended to the top of the main church, we both scuttled along the roof's perimeter, then crawled our way over to the other side, moving like a couple of cat burglars. Being Catholic I had mixed feelings about climbing around on the backside of a church, but I had no recollection of this being a sin. And in any case it was an Episcopal chapel and not a Catholic cathedral. And when we finally made it over to the front, Peter and I were rewarded with a breathtaking view of the city at night, with all of its tall buildings lit up.

Inspired, Peter produced a small pipe and a bag of pot.

"What about training rules?" I said.

"They only mention drinking." Peter shrugged.

"OK, but not too much," I suggested. "After all, we still have to climb down."

There is something profound about the stillness of a spring night, when you can almost feel the plants regenerating. Then again, it could have just been the pot.

For a while we just sat there in silence.

"So you think I'm too high?" Peter finally asked, out of the blue.

"What?" I said.

"My stroke rating," he clarified.

"Oh, right. Well, maybe a bit, but what do I know? After all, I'm only a sculler," I confessed.

"Well, you can always just tell me if I get going too fast," he said.

"OK, it's a deal."

More silence fell between us for a while, having solved this problem as if it were trivial. Of course I suspected that the debate might surface again during the heat of a race, where negotiation would be more difficult.

"The city looks so close from here," I said. "It almost looks like you could leap right over to it."

"Except for the small problem of the thirty-foot drop," Peter pointed out.

"Yeah, but I suppose that's just our perception of reality," I mused, starting to manifest the effects of the marijuana.

"I think it's called the law of gravity," Peter chided.

"Right. But sometimes I wonder if you could ever defy the laws of physics with blind faith."

"Really?" Peter asked, giving me a quizzical look.

We both had a fondness for the mystical worlds of Hermann Hesse and Carlos Castaneda, so I knew that Peter could at least entertain a brief discussion on this front.

"OK, then, let me ask you something," Peter said. "I mean, you're religious and all, right?"

"Well, my mother wanted me to be a priest," I admitted.

"I guess that qualifies you," Peter said.

We both laughed. "Fire away," I said.

"Do you really think that if you had that sort of . . . um . . . faith, and you stepped off this roof, you could walk right through the air?"

"I suppose so," I said. "I mean, theoretically."

"But how would that work?" Peter asked. I couldn't tell if he was genuinely curious or just high.

"I'm really not sure," I admitted. "Maybe some divine force would come up and support you."

"Huh," Peter said, drifting off into his own reverie.

"Anyway, let's not try it out tonight," I suggested.

"Agreed," he said.

We sat in suspended thought and silence for a while longer, mulling it over and just gazing at the city lights below. Then, having conjectured the nature of divinity and our place within it, we made our descent back down to Earth. Getting down, curiously enough, was a bit harder than going up, but thankfully we made it safely without incident.

After all, we had a race the next day: Columbia University in New York City.

Chapter Seventeen

Culture Clash at Columbia

"Take it down!" I shouted at Peter in between breaths that felt more like convulsions.

We'd come off the line at a forty-two and settled (if you wanted to call it that) to a thirty-eight. We were out ahead of Columbia by a length, but it wasn't pretty. And—at least based on the burning sensation in my lungs—it wasn't sustainable. Our beautiful Schoenbrod was checking badly between strokes, and every time I came up to the catch, I could see Heidi getting jerked around like a bobblehead in the stern.

We were rowing scared—not entirely a surprise after our unsettling warm-up on the Harlem River. Nearly as soon as we'd put our boat into the brown waters of the Spuyten Duyvil, our urban rowing odyssey began. The little creek connected the Harlem to the mighty Hudson, and farther downstream, where we headed to get to the starting line, the eight-mile channel of brown water joined the tidal estuary of the East River. Tidal means tides, and tides mean current. We were used to dealing with current on the Connecticut River, of course, but not the big tidal fluctuations that move through narrow, man-made channels.

Fourteen bridges line the Harlem, which is bounded on either side by rock walls, old buildings, and the Hudson railway line. In the 1970s it was also littered with trash of every shape and form imaginable. Since the 1700s, people had been using the river for shipping and waste disposal, which severely affected its water quality.

A half mile below the Columbia boathouse, we'd entered a straight stretch of water, boxed in by high seawalls. Coaching launches shot by us, throwing up massive wakes, which then bounced off these walls and made the river a virtual wash box. As we stopped to let the turbulence subside, Heidi took a rough inventory of all the flotsam and jetsam in the river, which included old tires and huge pieces of driftwood. She eyed these obstacles warily and then noticed a bunch of street kids hanging out next to the rail line, looking down at us with interest.

"Aw, look at those cute kids," Heidi said, and waved.

A few of them waved back. Then they started to pelt us with rocks. Most of the sharp stones landed harmlessly in the water, but one managed to hit our fiberglass hull, making a loud *thwack*.

"Start rowing—NOW!" Heidi shouted, losing her composure and quickly abandoning the formality of rowing commands. After twenty hard strokes we seemed to be in the clear and stopped once again to practice our racing starts, but from that moment on none of us kept our eyes in the boat.

"Did you hear the story about the Harvard crew that rowed here a few years back?" Peter asked.

"No . . .," Heidi replied.

"Never mind—I probably shouldn't tell you."

"C'mon," I chimed in. "Spit it out."

"Well, rumor has it they don't come here anymore because of what happened."

"What?!" Heidi said.

"Well, supposedly a cinderblock was dropped off one of these bridges and it smashed right through the wooden hull, barely missing an oarsman's legs."

"OK, great. Did you really have to tell me that?" Heidi said.

"You asked," Peter laughed. He was from Philly after all, which had its own history of class warfare between the haves and have-nots.

Rock throwing aside, we were feeling pretty pleased with ourselves after beating Coast Guard the previous week, especially since we'd been the only Trinity Crew to notch a victory that day. But Columbia was part of the Ivy League, and that put them in a different category. Their program had existed since 1895, and even though the Harlem River was clearly due for a makeover, Columbia still had the historical clout of a rowing dynasty. Earlier that day I'd taken a quick peek at the old photos in the Gould-Remmer Boathouse, which showcased impressive university crews dating back for decades.

Normally one of the benefits of rowing at an established regatta, hosted by an Ivy League crew program, is that things tend to go smoothly. After all, these folks have done it all before and worked out all the kinks that might bedevil a boat race. Whether the Harlem River was cursed or we simply came on a bad day was impossible to say, but all sorts of things started to go wrong. Just like at Coast Guard, both our varsity heavyweight and lightweight crews narrowly lost their races, and our freshman heavies trailed by a full length. Now it was once again up to us.

Because of the strong current and the lack of stake boats, many of the races actually started well past the starting line, which lay just beyond the Alexander Hamilton Bridge, where I-95 passes on the east side of Manhattan. A floating start, where the boats are lined up fairly, is hard enough to execute in still water; with a five-knot current, it becomes nearly impossible. We had a false start to begin with and had to row back under the bridge. Then the race official couldn't seem to get the boats lined up, and we drifted back beyond the bridge.

Exasperated, the umpire finally called out to Heidi that he would execute a countdown start, which we had never practiced before.

"10-9-8-7-6-5-4-3-2-1. Ready all, ROW!" he shouted.

Off we went, with the current behind us, tearing our blades through the filthy brown water. I yelled at Peter to settle down, just before I began to hyperventilate. Then I tried to relax and establish a rhythm, but I had the distinct feeling that something bad was about to happen.

Suddenly I heard a kerplunk sound nearby, like a fish jumping out of the water. Then I heard something go whizzing over our heads.

"What the hell was that?" Heidi screamed.

"Holy crap!" Peter shouted. "It's those kids again!"

"Row harder!" Dak said.

Sure enough, not far from the spot where we'd first noticed them, the gang of local kids was lined up like a firing squad, pelting us with rocks. For them, taking potshots at a bunch of wealthy college brats was probably the highlight of their weekend. Or maybe they were just bored. I'd actually been raised in a few neighborhoods where rock fights were not uncommon, so I knew what was happening wasn't personal. We were simply on their turf, and they were defending it.

Needless to say, our stroke rating never settled down and we sprinted the entire way down the course, beating Columbia by a length. Despite the victory, it didn't feel like a well-rowed race, and when we took our boat out of the water, it was covered with a layer of black slime. We decided not to throw Heidi in. Instead Coach Poole borrowed some kerosene and rags from the Columbia boatman, and we scrubbed the hull until it was white again.

Unbelievably our old coxswain, Phillip Poupé, suddenly appeared on the dock, standing arm-in-arm with his new girlfriend. He was smartly dressed in a black peacoat and Greek fisherman's cap, looking quite smug.

"Nice race, buttheads," he said.

"Phil—what the hell are you doing here?" I asked. "I thought you hated rowing."

"I do," he said. "But I live in Manhattan, and I'm spending the weekend at my parents' penthouse. Lindsay and I thought we'd take in the races."

Everyone else on the team ignored him as we continued to wipe down our boat. After all, Phil had quit the team last fall under less than friendly terms, and in crew that never sits well.

"I see all you could get was a girl to replace me," Phil said. His girlfriend giggled, and Heidi bit her tongue.

"You know, there's something that I always wanted to give you when you were our coxswain," Dak said.

"Oh really?" Phil said. "What's that?"

"A wedgie!" he said loudly.

As if on command, we all dropped our kerosene rags and grabbed him by the edge of his undershorts. Peacoat and all, we hauled him over to the river and threw him into the dirty waters of Spuyten Duyvil.

"You b-bastards!" he screamed, when he finally bobbed to the surface. His black curls were now plastered to his head, and he looked like a river rat.

His girlfriend giggled, and our victory was complete.

Chapter Eighteen

Henry Cropsey's Hidden Talent

The rain came down steady and cold as we sat at the starting line of our first home regatta. After a brief warm-up, including a few racing starts, we'd backed ourselves into one of the anchored stake boats and set ourselves up across from our opponent—the University of Rhode Island (URI). Rumor had it that they weren't that good, so we were hoping to get the race over with quickly. Other than heavy wind there are few conditions more challenging for oarsmen than cold rain. Even snow is arguably better. Rowing clothes only do so much to keep out precipitation of any sort, and as freshmen we were less prepared than most. And so, as we waited for the umpire to send us off, we sat there feeling more and more miserable. By the time the boats were aligned, I estimated that we'd added at least ten pounds of extra weight to our boat, both with our wet clothes and the standing water in the hull.

"THE HANDS ARE DOWN . . . READY ALL, ROW!" the umpire finally barked. We punched our blades into the heavy, cold water and churned our way up to a rate of forty-two. The URI frosh lightweights matched us stroke for stroke, and we were off to a clean, fast start. After winding it up for a high twenty, Peter dropped us into a solid cadence of thirty-two. Things were looking good.

"I've got a half boat length lead," Heidi shouted, urging us forward.

Nobody felt that much like racing, and a few people were still sick from the week before. I could hear Henry Phillips wheezing behind me, and I felt my own lungs give their usual protest at my demand for extra oxygen.

We'd barely cleared the first five hundred meters when suddenly our boat started fishtailing wildly, and pitching from left to right.

"What the hell?" Wean yelled from the bow.

"It's the fin!" Peter cried out. "We've lost our fin!"

"OK, OK, WEIGH ENOUGH!" Heidi finally shouted, when piloting the boat became untenable.

In collegiate rowing at the time, there was an equipment breakage rule. A race could be rerowed if the broken equipment in question happened within the first one hundred meters, and the breakage was not due to user error. After that allowance, however, it was simply tough luck. If someone jumped his slide or jammed a shirttail under his seat, or crabbed, it didn't matter. So we just sat there in our disabled boat and watched our rivals from URI row by us and continue down the course, unchallenged.

"Well, that blows," Peter said.

"Yep," I agreed.

"OK, shake it off, guys. Let's take it home," Heidi said.

We paddled back to the dock halfheartedly, landed, and started to remove our oars from the oarlocks. On the one hand, we were relieved to be off the water and out of the rain, but on the other hand, our bodies felt disrupted from doing the task they'd been trained to do day after day. The varsity crews were just preparing to boat, and some of them looked over at us, curious and puzzled by our early return to the dock.

"Well, did you win?" Carl Rox asked expectantly.

Heidi shook her head and explained what had happened.

"Tough luck, little lickers!" Mongo said. "Equipment breakage is a bit like interrupted sex," he offered.

"Exactly," Carl Rox agreed.

We pulled our boat out of the water in silence.

"Buttheads," Wean mumbled, just loudly enough for them to hear.

The only virtue of sitting out during a regatta is that you finally notice all of the other teams that make up a rowing program. During normal circumstances you are mostly focused on yourself, and this is particularly the case for freshman rowers. All told the Trinity Crew program was made up of nine boats, and that afternoon nearly the entire flotilla was out on the Connecticut River. Our varsity heavy four plowed their way to victory, right after our fiasco, followed by a decent showing by the JV lights. The varsity heavyweights got passed at the fifteen hundred–meter mark, but fought back and barely lost to URI in the final sprint. And in the final race on the men's side, the varsity lightweight squads rowed out of a two-seat deficit to end up winning handily by eight seconds.

But the real heroes of the day were the Trinity women, who were racing both URI and the University of Massachusetts (UMass). Like the frosh lights, the varsity gals had been on an undefeated tear all season, and they surprised the favorite, the UMass, beating them handily by open water. The third-place crew, URI, was a full forty-five seconds behind them. The women's novices won as well.

"We totally shellacked those guys!" Cynda Davis announced after the race. "I mean, did you see the look on their coach's face? And URI completely pooched."

"All right, all right," the women's coach, Andy Sanders, said. "Let's not get too high on ourselves . . ."

But Davis would have plenty of time to crow about their victory when she wrote up the race results for the *Trinity Tripod* the following day, comparing her boat to none other than the illustrious Harvard men's heavyweight crew:

WOMEN'S CREW CRUSHES UMASS AND URI
by Cynda Davis
A short time ago, Harvard's heavyweight crew swept the prestigious San Diego Crew Classic. Being a much smaller crew, they were not expected to win the event and, in general, were not expected to be the powerhouse that they have always been. As one newspaper reported, they merely led from start to finish. So too, Trinity's women crews were not expected to best the UMass women. Coach Sanders was confident; he referred to the Harvard victory in San Diego and made it clear that Trinity had to control the race from the start. Both the varsity eight and the novice eight did just that . . .

The piece went on to articulate the specifics of the grand victory, and then concluded:

As Trinity was carrying their shell off the dock, the UMass coach, president of the National Women's Rowing Association, reluctantly voiced an "Excellent race, girls."

Trinity was supposed to be their easy race, but tides turn with each passing boat. Perhaps next year they will be a little more apprehensive of the fate that awaits them on the Connecticut . . .

"Oh dear," Dak said, as he read the article aloud to me the next day at breakfast. His father was an economist who wrote a column for the *Wall Street Journal*, and this bit of journalism in the *Trinity Tripod* wasn't quite up to his standards.

"A bit of hyperbole, perhaps?" Henry Cropsey asked, with his face buried in a bowl of oatmeal. Henry sat two seat in the freshman heavyweight boat, but sometimes he liked to sit with us, and we liked him to. Soft-spoken and thoughtful, he had a genuine curiosity about other people and knowing what they thought. A few bits of oats stuck to his grizzled chin when he finally looked up and gave a crooked smile.

"I wonder what she would have written if they'd lost," he mused.

"Uh ... probably a lot less," Dak said, chuckling.

"What can anyone say when they lose?" I asked, still thinking about what happened to us the day before.

"Well, we didn't exactly lose ..." Dak said.

"Yeah, but we didn't win, either," I pointed out.

"Well, my boat *definitely* lost," Henry said. "And we actually haven't won a race all season."

Dak and I both fell silent. We hadn't even been thinking about the heavies.

"How do you deal with losing?" I said. "I mean, how do you keep your spirits up?"

"That's easy," Henry said. "I play the bagpipes."

Dak laughed. "You're joking," he said.

Henry smiled again, and his eyes twinkled.

"I'm actually going to play tonight, if you guys want to join me."

"I'll pass," Dak said. "Homework."

"Where do you play?" I asked.

"You'll see," he said. "Meet me in the Bancroft Arch after dinner."

⁓

Henry arrived right on time, just as the carillons had finished chiming in the upper reaches of the chapel. He was dressed in a houndstooth jacket and gray woolen pants; he looked more like a professor than an undergraduate. It wasn't raining anymore, so I only had on jeans and my crew jacket.

"Where to, Henry?" I asked.

"Well, eventually, we're heading to the cemetery," he replied. "It's the only place I can play without annoying anyone. But first I have to duck into my dorm so I can change into my kilt."

"Really?" I said.

"Yes, it's traditional," Henry said. "The kilt, that is."

After Henry got himself all geared up, we marched off across the main quad, heading toward fraternity row. At the bottom of Summit Avenue lay an old Episcopal graveyard, where we'd once met Harry Graves before our big night of drinking at the Nutshell. Halfway across the quad, we bumped straight into Heidi and a rower from the freshman women's team named Laurie Shields. They were tossing a Frisbee back and forth, looking bored.

"What are you guys doing?" they asked, glancing at Henry's attire.

"I'm going to practice my bagpipes in the cemetery," he said, matter-of-factly. "Want to join us?"

They looked at each other blankly. Heidi just shrugged.

"Sure, why not," Laurie said.

"Wonderful," Henry remarked, then winked at me as if to indicate that he'd scored us a double date.

As we passed the chapel and then the campus gate on Summit Street, Henry pointed in the direction of St. Anthony's Hall. "Just over there is a place known as Gallows Hill, where some women were supposedly executed for being witches in the seventeenth century."

"What?" Laurie asked. "Is that really true?"

"It might be," Henry said, and smiled.

Laurie and Heidi just looked at each other and frowned, falling back behind us a little.

"Way to set the romantic mood, Henry," I said to him.

By the time we reached the cemetery, it was nearly dark. Aside from a single streetlight, there wasn't much to guide us through the maze of gravestones. Heidi and Laurie seemed a bit less keen about the entire venture as they looked around for a place to perch. But with his legs firmly planted in a patch of open grass, Henry began to play a few warm-up notes, and then he launched into a familiar tune.

"Hey, I know that song," Laurie said. "It's 'Danny Boy'!"

"Yes. Very funny, Henry," I said.

"I thought you might like it," he said when he finished. His eyes twinkled again, seeking approval.

"It's nice, but that contraption is awfully loud," Heidi said, looking around to see if we'd attracted any attention.

"It's loud enough to wake up the dead," Laurie agreed.

"Or the campus police," I chimed in.

"I'm still thinking about those poor witches," Laurie mused. "To be honest, I'm sort of getting the heebie-jeebies, standing here."

"Let's head back to the dorms," Heidi suggested. "It's getting kind of late anyway."

Henry nodded with indifference. His mouth fell back onto the bagpipes, and ignoring our departure, he began to play another song. Gazing straight ahead he seemed to enter some sort of a trance, so we left him there, playing to his captive audience.

"Well, that was totally weird," Laurie said, as the three of us made our way back to the campus gate, which was just about to get locked for the night.

"Yeah, I guess bagpipes are kind of cool," I observed, "but they're a little bit like parents—there's only so much of them you can take!"

Laurie laughed and then peeled away from us, jogging back to her dorm. Heidi and I continued back to Jarvis together.

"I think she might like you a little bit," Heidi said.

"Really?" I asked. "How can you tell?"

She shrugged. "I just can."

"So, does that count as a first date?" I asked.

Heidi smiled.

"I think it's more like a first encounter," she said.

"A pretty odd one, I guess."

"Yeah, but certainly an improvement from drawing letters on Porgy's butt," she pointed out.

I laughed as I punched in the door code to Jarvis.

As soon as we stepped inside, we heard a commotion in the hallway above us and then bumped straight into my roommate Jim, looking distressed.

"Quick. Grab your guitar," he said. "Snibble's about to get himself killed!"

CHAPTER NINETEEN

Football Players

DeTucci was staring down Snibble again, and he had him cornered up against the fire escape door. Their eyes were locked together in combat mode, and every muscle on Snibble's body seemed to be twitching in fear. DeTucci was Mike DeTucci, the star tackle on the Trinity football team, and Snibble was John Snibble, a child prodigy physics major and self-proclaimed super nerd. Both guys had an inherent dislike for the other, and occasionally the tension between them erupted into twisted dramas—usually on a weekend night.

When I arrived on the scene, several guys had already come out of their rooms to watch the show, and an expectation of violence hung in the air.

"Now Tuche, take it easy," Mike's roommate Butchy cautioned. He was also a varsity football player. "You don't want to get kicked off the team for next season!"

"That's right, Tuche, take it easy now," Snibble echoed. A slight lisp trailed off of his effeminate lips, which came to rest in an uneasy smile.

He wore thick wire-rimmed glasses, under which lay his puffy eyes; high-waisted jeans; and black Keds sneakers. He had a bad case of body odor, and the grungy T-shirt that he never took off said, "Space: The Final Frontier." When he wasn't studying, Snibble could usually be found playing Alien Invaders in the cafeteria lounge, where he currently held the record for the highest score. He was tall and gawky, and there was no mass to his muscle. Nevertheless he was now bravely holding his arms out in front of him, in a mock karate gesture against DeTucci. His long, bony fingers were visibly shaking.

Suddenly Snibble flinched, and DeTucci rushed at him like a mad bull, grabbing him around the legs. Snibble pitched forward, falling over DeTucci's massive back, and before he could react, he found himself airborne and flying backward. In one motion DeTucci hoisted Snibble's long, skinny body up off the ground and slammed it up against the fire escape door. The impact made a loud thud, and Snibble wheezed as the wind was knocked out of him.

"Oh, that had to hurt," said Butchy, grinning nervously at the assembled group of dorm rats.

Most of the guys watching weren't serious athletes or nerds, but just a bunch of average college lay-a-bouts who played high-stakes poker every weekend night. Nobody had really wanted the fight to happen, but no one had tried to stop it either. If truth be told, almost everyone on the floor secretly mocked Snibble behind his back, often competing to see who could best imitate his lisp. They weren't happy to see him get humiliated like this, but there was something riveting about violence that now held their full attention. Mostly they were simply relieved that it wasn't one of them getting pummeled. And by watching the weakest one in the dorm get taken out, they assumed they were somehow given immunity.

Filled with pent-up rage and aggression, Mike DeTucci was the perfect guy for the job. Football season was over, and he needed a physical release of some sort. Snibble was simply a human tackle sled. Pinned up against the wall like a bug, John was still trying valiantly to maintain his composure—but this was no video game. His glasses were starting to fog up, as the reality of the situation set in.

"Quick, get your guitar," Jim repeated.

I'd seen DeTucci go at Snibble before, and it usually didn't end well. On the one hand, this was just a bizarre exercise in play-acting—jock against nerd—but often when guys took out their aggressions in mock battles, it wasn't really a game. Sports, at least, had some rules, but a free-for-all fight was an invitation for disaster. And having been on the receiving end, back in high school, I knew firsthand how it would feel for Snibble. At the moment it was impossible to say whether Mike DeTucci had any real control at all either, for he had clearly given himself over to his performance. He had become the beast, and Snibble was his prey. Where was the RA, you might ask? Ours was busy courting a freshman coed. So I ran back to my room and pulled my guitar out of its case.

When I returned, DeTucci still had Snibble pinned against the wall, and his face was now red and on the verge of tears.

"Take it easy, Tuche," Butchy whispered, trying to calm down his roommate. The corridor was now completely quiet, and I could tell that a deep part of Mike was no longer reachable by words.

I played the first few lines of "Dueling Banjos," from the movie *Deliverance*. Like magic, all eyes were suddenly diverted toward me.

"Listen, Tuche," Butchy said. "Boyne is playing your favorite song!"

I plucked the first few notes again, imitating the banjo part, then strummed loudly, issuing the guitar's response. Now I had the crowd's attention, so I wound it up, playing faster, fingerpicking my way through the bluegrass tune, and strumming loudly in between the notes. A few people started clapping to the quickening beat.

Slowly DeTucci lowered Snibble to the ground and turned around to listen for himself. The anger that had changed his face into a deadpan mask slowly melted as he began to listen to the music. Then he smiled, and I knew I had him.

"Yee haw!" he shouted. "Play it faster, now, Boyne!"

I rapped my knuckles against the steel strings and picked the melody line still faster. Everyone was engaged in the song now, and even Snibble had started to smile again, regaining his dignity and pretending that my entrance and the music was all part of the night's performance.

Suddenly the RA showed up, having been told of the commotion.

"What's going on here?" he asked, surveying the room. One of the trash barrels had tipped over in the melee. His eyes finally landed on John Snibble, who was busy tucking his ripped T-shirt back into his pants.

"Nothing happening here, chief," DeTucci said. "We're all just having a little fun!"

"Are you sure?" the RA said, directing the question at John.

"That's right," Snibble agreed. "Good clean fun!"

No one else said a word, of course, because those were simply the rules. After I finished playing, most of the guys broke off to resume their nightly poker game, while the rest of us got ready to turn in for the night.

"I'll see you later," Mike DeTucci said, pointing a finger at Snibble.

"Not unless I see you first," John shot back, smiling his goofy smile.

Snibble walked back to his room. He had a weird, gangly gate that wasn't quite normal. I started to leave, too, when Mike stopped me.

"Hey Boyne, come in here for a second," he said, motioning me toward his room.

I'd never really hung out with Mike and Butchy before, mainly because they were football players. You didn't mess with them, and they didn't mess with you. Crew people were weird, but football jocks seemed to hold themselves even further apart from the rest of campus. My dad had played football in high school and college, but I'd never really bothered to try and understand the nature of the game or the guys who played it.

Their room was full of football awards and trophies, and it was remarkably clean for a couple of serious athletes.

"Can you teach me how to play that thing?" Mike said, motioning toward the guitar in my hands.

"Ah—sure," I said, relieved at the reason for his invitation.

I sat down and perched the guitar on my lap and showed him a few basic chords. Tuche was a fast learner, and after a few minutes he was struggling his way through a serviceable chorus of "The House of the Rising Sun."

"Ha ha!" Butchy laughed. "Tuche, you sound like Bob Dylan."

Mike handed back the guitar, and as I got up to leave, I noticed a fly rod case sitting in a corner of the room.

"You fly fish?" I said incredulously.

"Yeah," Mike said. "I love it."

"He's a total pro," Butchy confirmed.

"I've tried it," I said, "but I'm not that good."

"Well, let's go fishing sometime this spring," Mike said. "I'll show you some tricks, in exchange for guitar lessons."

"It's a deal," I agreed.

Butchy followed me outside.

"Hey, Boyne, you and the other guys won't tell anyone about the, ah—incident—tonight?" he said.

"Of course not," I said.

Butchy nodded and smiled.

"What you have to understand about Tuche is that he can't entirely control himself," Butchy explained. "But that's what makes him dangerous and great as an athlete."

"I think I get it," I said. "My father played football."

He nodded again and patted me on the back.

"That's good. That's real good. Thanks."

As I walked back to my room, I began to remember some of the old stories my father had told me about his own college football days, playing on scholarship, and how he'd been kicked out of school at least once or twice for bad conduct. Was it the sport itself that produced this behavior? Further back I remembered him mentioning how he and his older brother had been beaten up by their own dad on several occasions. It was clearly not something that he wanted to dwell on, but still wanted me to know, perhaps to explain his own moments of anger. Needless to say I was quite familiar with the Jekyll and Hyde transformation that had come over DeTucci, for I'd seen it growing up, with other football players. Now, suddenly, I felt more sympathetic with them. It didn't negate their bad behavior, but it certainly helped to explain it.

Back in the sanctuary of my own room, I found Jim stretched out on his bunk, looking over an issue of *Track and Field*.

"Nice job," he said, when I closed the door.

"Thanks," I said, putting my guitar away.

"You know, I think I'm going to try out for the track team this spring," Jim said. "I really want to do the high jump."

Trinity College quadrangle, Hartford, Connecticut.

Trinity College, Hartford, Connecticut.

Trinity women's varsity eight rowing at the Head of the Charles, 1977.
ANDY ANDERSON

The Trinity freshman lightweight crew, spring 1979 (author, second from right). CHARLIE POOLE

Freshman lightweight eight, Head of the Charles, 1978 (author in the two seat). PETER TYSON

Rowing plaque at Trinity College.
CHRISTINA BLEYER

Trinity men's unlikely coxswain, Heidi Wittwer, who had been cut from the women's team that year. HEIDI WITTWER

Shawn Boyne, the author's sister, rowing at Mount Holyoke College, circa 1977. SHAWN BOYNE

The Trinity freshman heavyweight and lightweight teams, with Coach Charlie Poole. CHARLIE POOLE

The closing sprint. Coming into the final twenty strokes of the frosh light finals, Dad Vails, 1979. PETER TYSON

The Dad Vail Regatta starting line, with anchored stake boats.
PETER TYSON

Trinity over Coast Guard, by .05 second. PETER TYSON

The stern four, standing with their coach on the awards dock (right to left: Charlie Poole, Peter Tyson, the author, Henry Phillips, and Richard Malabre). PETER TYSON

Rowing away with the gold. PETER TYSON

On the awards dock. PETER TYSON

Boathouse Row, Philadelphia, at night. ERIC DRESSER

"Interesting idea," I said. "Maybe you can practice by taking over the top bunk for the rest of the semester and leaping up to it every night."

"Nice try," he said, putting down his magazine and closing his eyes. "Shut off the light when you are ready."

After I put my guitar back in its case, I clambered up the ladder and went straight to sleep, with the sounds of *Deliverance* still echoing in my ears.

CHAPTER TWENTY

The Winds of Waramaug

If every race is like a performance, then each one is also just a dress rehearsal for the big finale at the end of the season—the National Championships.

The Lake Waramaug Invitational was our last competition before the Dad Vail Regatta, which was considered the national championship for small colleges at that time. Most of the crews attending that Philadelphia event hailed from the Eastern seaboard, but not all. Marietta and Minnesota would make the long trip from the South and Midwest, and the University of British Columbia might bring a well-prepared Thunderbird crew all the way across the country to try their luck on Boathouse Row.

Before the Vails, however, we first had to duel against Williams, Ithaca, and Marist at Waramaug—three small liberal arts colleges with well-established crew programs. What many people in rowing don't realize is that some of these small New England colleges, including Bowdoin and Amherst, originally helped form the backbone of collegiate rowing back in the 1870s, using coxless six-oared shells. It was only in 1876 that Harvard and Yale introduced coxed eights and decided to race four miles in New London.

As soon as we disembarked from our Peter Pan bus, all the Trinity squads assembled and started to busy ourselves with prerace preparations, eager to show what we could do. Trinity was a Division III school, but its sports teams often went above and beyond this designation, and with Norm Graf by our side, we carried ourselves with a sense of pride and dignity. All except Mongo, that is, who hopped off the bus and promptly released an enormous fart.

"Jowurski, I believe the porta potties are that way," Graf pointed out.

The lake looked deceptively bucolic at first inspection, with gently forested shores and a grassy bank lined with picnic benches. The launching area was part of a state park, and it had good views for spectators at the finish line. Overall the rural feel of the place was a welcome relief for those of us who had endured the long winter and urban grind of Hartford.

"Far out! We're in the country now," Joe (Rhino) Rhineman announced in his mellow California voice.

Rhino was the four seat of our boat, and I'd begun to hang out with him more and more, even though he was a bit of an odd duck. With his blond curls and body-builder physique, he seemed more like a surfer dude than an oarsman, and his prerace meditation practice had recently earned him another nickname—Karma Joe. I'd come to appreciate his laid-back attitude, though, because it was radically different from the uptight East Coast vibe.

Heidi herded us toward the shell trailer, and we carefully offloaded the two sections of our eight. Dak was in charge of bolting them together, first applying a thick coat of Vaseline to ensure the seam wouldn't leak. We soon got caught up in the ritual behaviors of prerace preparation—not only the necessary labors of rigging the boat, but also cleaning and coddling our seats and oar handles, not wanting them to jam or slip. Joe, however, soon wandered off and sat under a pine tree, while the rest of us glanced about nervously at the other teams and pretended to stretch.

"Hey Rhino," Wean called out, as he rolled his seat back and forth for the umpteenth time. "What are you doing over there—taking a dump?"

Everyone laughed.

"He's probably thinking about his old high school girlfriend," Porgy ventured.

"I don't think he had one!" Rob said.

"Ha ha!" Wean guffawed. "HEY JOE," he called out, "ARE YOU STILL A VIRGIN?"

We all laughed again.

"Actually, he is probably thinking about all the food he's going to eat after the season is over and he doesn't have to make weight," Henry Phillips offered.

No one responded, because the comment wasn't funny to a bunch of lightweights.

"OK, leave him alone," Dak said.

Joe continued to sit calmly under his pine tree, unaffected by all of the teasing. A gentle gust of wind blew lightly through his blond curls. He sat facing the lake, smiling like a tranquil Buddha.

Our other rivals had recently arrived—Ithaca, Williams, and Marist. Ithaca was just starting to unload their trailer, and the Ephmen, dressed in their trademark purple, were already rigging their boats. I looked over at the Ephs with some degree of envy, for Williams had been my first choice for college admission, but I didn't get in, even though I'd applied early decision.

Ithaca had never been on my shopping list of schools, maybe because it was so far north. But now, as I watched the Ithaca team joking and carrying on, I thought they looked cool in a Seattle grunge sort of way, years before that fashion trend became popular.

Instead of being all preppy or outfitted in team sweats, the Ithaca guys milled about in thermal shirts and wool caps, looking pretty laid back for a bunch of athletes. One of them mentioned a keg party happening later that day that he was definitely planning to attend, win or lose.

"Hey Joe," Wean said, when Rhino rejoined the group, "maybe you should have gone to Ithaca. Seriously. They seem like your kind of people."

"Wean, you know, you can be kind of a dick sometimes," Joe said.

Everyone laughed, because Joe had delivered the remark in such an unaggressive, offhanded way.

"Hey, Joe," I said, sidling up next to him. "If you don't mind me asking, what do you actually do when you meditate?"

Joe shrugged. "I just relax. Then I visualize our race and row two hundred perfect strokes," he said.

"Really? That's it?"

He nodded. "It's like making my own movie or creating a dream."

"Huh," I said. "But how does it feel when we are actually racing? I mean, don't you ever get stressed out that we are going to lose or catch a crab or something?"

"Not really. That's all negative crap. I'm pulling hard, of course, but I'm pretty relaxed about the whole racing business, because I figure what will be, will be. Right? So I'm really just trying to let it all happen the way I've imagined beforehand."

"Two hundred perfect strokes," I said.

"Exactly," Joe said.

I studied his face to see if he was putting me on, but he just gazed back with an innocent smile. If Joe had been a dog, he would have been a golden retriever, for there was absolutely no guile about him.

"Sometimes I even feel like there is this invisible cord attached to our bow, pulling us down the racecourse," he added, lowering his voice to a whisper.

"That's pretty cool," I said, even though I thought it was pretty weird.

"OK, LET'S GO. HANDS ON!" Heidi called out.

We dropped what we were doing and grabbed our boat.

Every waterway has its own character, but lakes are notably different from rivers. They can be bucolic and still in the early hours of the morning, but quite dangerous later in the day if the wind rises. And this is exactly what happened on Lake Waramaug that afternoon.

If you've never rowed in whitecaps before, it's not a pleasant experience. Ocean rowers laugh at what we call rough water, since they are used to getting buffeted about by much larger swells at sea. But a freshwater oarsman is generally not accustomed to anything larger than a foot-high wave, and the boats aren't really designed to handle anything more substantial. We'd swamped once before, of course, so we knew what it was like to deal with rough conditions. So after we put our boat in the water and tied in, we braced ourselves for a bumpy ride.

Waramaug had its own storied past as a rowing venue, but only recently had it started to be used for larger regattas. Before then it mainly had been used as a training ground for local high schools, Kent, East Kent, and the Gunnery. It had a fifteen hundred–meter stretch that was perfect for high school races, but in order to squeeze out an extra five hundred meters, college crews had to start right up against the shore.

We quickly sailed our way down to the starting line, aided by the tailwind, but when we stopped to spin, the boat would barely budge. The riggers creaked as the ports backed and starboards rowed, but we finally got it turned around and pointed directly into the wind. Four guys in fisherman's waders served as human stake boats, and each one grabbed the stern of a crew and tried to hold it fast. Williams was to our right, Marist and Ithaca were to starboard. We needed to get out ahead to avoid a crash, as there weren't any lane markers.

"C'mon," Heidi said, "let's take them off the line."

The umpire dropped the flag, since verbal commands were useless in the wind. Then the boats were off, oars swinging wildly in the messy chop. I could barely keep a blade full of water through the entire stroke, but nevertheless our heavyweight-size hull bobbed over the wave tops with surprising ease. After the first thirty strokes we had open water on the rest of the field, and we proceeded to blast our way forward. Ironically, the fact that we were rowing in a heavyweight shell worked to our advantage that day, because our boat had plenty of freeboard and didn't take on much water. The other teams were less fortunate.

When we finished, the next crew to come in behind us was Ithaca College—fifty-four seconds back. Marist trailed us by one minute four seconds. Williams didn't even finish. Spring boat races are usually won by margins of a few seconds, so this victory was nothing short of a walloping. As we derigged our boat and prepared to leave, the other crews came over and gave us their betting shirts. The purple one with the white W was especially pleasing to receive.

"That was way too easy," I said, admiring the purple T-shirt I'd just acquired from the Williams seven seat. "I almost feel badly for the other teams."

"Why? It's not really about them," Joe said.

"Right. It's about taking two hundred perfect strokes," I quoted.

Joe smiled. I had to admit, it was a great technique.

Suddenly Mongo and Carl Rox strode by, proudly clutching the two betting shirts they'd won like a pair of scalps. All the Trinity squads except the varsity lights had been victorious that day, and it made for a festive postrace atmosphere.

"YEAH, BABY!" they cried, holding the betting shirts up in front of our faces. Despite their moronic behavior, I was happy for them.

What I hadn't told anyone was that I'd been struggling with my energy levels ever since I'd been sick during spring break. Whatever strain of flu I'd fought off had partially remained in my system and continued to wreak havoc. I was down to about 140 pounds and always felt tired. At the Trinity health services office, the clinician had taken some of my blood and informed me that my white cell counts were totally depleted.

The recommendation was rest and time off from intense physical exertion.

Naturally, I couldn't do that.

On the bus ride back to Hartford, I quietly shared this information with Joe, along with my growing concern about being able to defeat Coast Guard again at the Dad Vails.

"Somehow I have to figure out how to make it through the last week of the season," I said.

Joe listened patiently.

"Dude, you don't have to try so hard. Remember, you create your own reality."

"I guess," I said.

"There's no guesswork about it. The question is—can you imagine us winning at the Vails?" he asked.

"Yes," I said. "Definitely."

"Then focus on that outcome, and it will happen."

I closed my eyes and drifted off to sleep, hoping that Karma Joe was right.

CHAPTER TWENTY-ONE

The City of Brotherly Love

Ah, Philadelphia in springtime. No, it isn't Paris, but there are some similarities. Both cities have rivers that run through them. And like the Seine, the olive-colored river that runs through Philly is peppered with random parks and statuary. Numerous old bridges traverse the Schuylkill, some of them made famous by the local oarsman and painter Thomas Eakins, who studied abroad at L'École des Beaux-Arts. Most of the serious artwork, of course, is housed in the Philadelphia Art Museum, but there are outdoor sculptures scattered about the area near Boathouse Row, itself one of the most visually stunning examples of rowing architecture in the United States.

As our charter bus crossed over the Girard Bridge, we got a quick bird's-eye view of this historic waterway, the one we'd soon be racing on. Then we banked a right onto Kelly Drive, which brought us down to water level. Already the Schuylkill was awash with other crews, and as we drove along the east bank of the river, Peter played tour guide, identifying blade colors of local clubs—Penn AC, Vesper, Fairmount, and his old high school crew, Haverford. He also pointed out noteworthy landmarks like the Strawberry Mansion Bridge, which marked the fifteen hundred–meter pivot point of the dogleg racecourse.

"And there's the statue of Jack Kelly," Peter said.

We spied a bronze statue of a giant oarsman in a single scull, perched just before the grandstands that marked the finish line.

"Who the hell is that?" Rob asked.

"Just some dead dude," Porgy chimed in.

"No, not just some dead dude," Carl Rox bellowed. "Kelly was one of the most famous oarsmen of all time!"

"Yeah, show some respect, dumbass frosh," Mongo added.

"I've heard of Grace Kelly," Heidi offered.

"That's his daughter," Bill Windridge said. "Her performance in *Rear Window* was outstanding, and of course now she's the Princess of Monaco who—."

"Look, there are the steps that Rocky ran up!" Wean cut in.

We were now passing by the Philadelphia Art Museum.

"Dude, we *definitely* need to run up those bad boys before our race!" Joe said.

Clearly Rocky Balboa was more important than Jack Kelly.

＊

What happens when you put sixty oarsmen in one hotel? Add eighteen female rowers into the mix, and you have a recipe for misadventure. The Trinity women had finally joined us for our final trip, having mostly followed their own schedule during the season. The women's varsity eight, stroked by Cynda Davis, had gone undefeated, and just like us they had high hopes to win big.

They referred to themselves as "The Sultans of Swing," and all the way down to Philly, they blasted the Dire Straits song again and again, until someone finally wrestled their boom box away from them and tossed the cassette tape out the window, replacing it with the Rolling Stones classic "Shattered." By the time we entered the

City of Brotherly Love, everyone had joined in with the ragged voice of Mick Jagger, who whipped us into an R&B frenzy:

Laughter, joy, and loneliness and sex and sex and sex and sex
Look at me, I'm in tatters
I'm a shattered
Shattered

When the bus stopped, Norm Graf stood up and tried to restore order.

"OK, everyone! Now I know this is our first coed outing of the season . . ."

Hoots and hollers rang out, not all of which came from the men's team.

" . . . this is also our last race, and we have a real chance to win the Jack Bratten Point Trophy—but only if everyone pulls hard and works to his or her potential."

More cheers were heard, but the message quickly sank in and delivered its sobering effect.

"And so, while I know that this will be a grave disappointment for some of you to hear, I want you all to abstain from any sex this weekend, which has been scientifically proven to reduce sports performance."

Graf glared at us, trying to keep a straight face while groans, snickering, and other sounds followed. "That's bullshit," someone muttered.

"WELL, HELL'S BELLS!" Cynda Davis boomed from the back of the bus. "I think I can keep a lid on things, if all of you boys can manage to keep your hands off of *me!*"

"AHHH! Let me out of here!" a chorus of male voices shouted, and the stampede to exit the bus commenced.

At the hotel I was slated to room with Peter, and because of his contacts at Undine Barge, Trinity had been granted permission to boat from that prestigious old club, situated at number 13 Boathouse Row. After a quick change of clothes, we all ran back down to the river, dodging cars on Kelly Drive, and began to rig our shell. It was time to learn the ways of the Schuylkill. Other crews were doing the same, and Boathouse Row had quickly become a virtual beehive of activity, with a slew of oarsmen and coaches promenading along the sidewalk, marshaled by Dad Vail race officials dressed in bright-yellow jackets. They certainly had their hands full, with 235 crews and 1,650 oarsmen from 54 colleges in attendance that weekend.

On the way to our trailer to fetch our oars, I managed to bump straight into none other than Samuel Caluso, who was walking around Kelly Drive with one of his Coast Guard teammates. We both stopped dead in our tracks and stared each other up and down for a few long seconds. I started to turn around when Caluso held up his hand and walked over, acting as if we were old buddies.

"Hey, Boyne. How's it going? This is my teammate, Gerald."

I shook Gerald's hand. They both had crew cuts in the military fashion.

"What's up with you?" I asked.

"Well, we haven't lost a race since we met you guys back in April."

"That's great," I said. "Neither have we."

There was an uncomfortable silence. Then Gerald wandered off, leaving the two of us alone.

"Hey, I know there's been some bad feeling between us in the past," Caluso said, "but let's let bygones be bygones." He stuck out his hand and then added, "May the best boat win."

I stared at his hand for a second, as if it were a poisonous snake.

"OK," I said, and we locked hands.

For a nanosecond I entertained the notion that the guy who had tortured me all through high school had finally owned up to his past misdeeds. But the sentiment didn't match up with Caluso's grip, which was hard and aggressive and not at all friendly. Or was it just my imagination? It takes a lot of work to dislike someone, and maybe it was time to let it go, whatever the real sentiment might be.

"See you at the finish line," he said, grinning.

"Not unless I see you first," I said.

I rejoined my frosh lightweight squad, and we shoved off from Undine to take our first and only practice row. At first we were totally preoccupied with the challenge of trying to negotiate our way through the logjam of other crews, but once we rowed upstream and crossed over to the far shore, things grew quieter and we began to enjoy distant views of old mansions in Fairmount Park, which sat on grassy hummocks and suggested a time gone by. Farther upstream, past the starting line, lay the working-class village of East Falls, where Jack Kelly had grown up, and the wilder splendor of the river's upper reaches.

I thought about a lot of things during that practice row, but none of them really mattered, save one. And as Heidi called our minds back into the boat and we started our prerace sequence of starts and short pieces, everything quickly washed away in the one desire and the ultimate reason to row—to win.

Chapter Twenty-Two

Prerace Rituals

The night before a championship regatta, no one gets any sleep. The mental anticipation of racing is bad enough, but there is also the physical jitteriness that comes from tapering down during the last days heading into the final race. Charlie had purposefully begun to restrict the volume of our power strokes during practices, aside from a few random racing starts and twenties, and we were wound up like a bunch of racehorses who hadn't been allowed to gallop.

To try and take our minds off of what lay ahead, he had accepted an invitation from Peter Tyson's parents for a team dinner at their house that evening, some thirty minutes outside the city. Before dinner, however, we had a few hours to kill, so Peter and I sat around our hotel room and chatted with his younger sister, Lisa, who had stopped by for a brief visit. She lazily sprawled herself out on Peter's bed and glanced at the pictures in the Dad Vail program, then began to lament the ennui of finishing her senior year at Agnes Irwin, a local girl's high school. While the two siblings were catching up, the hotel phone beside the bed rang, so I answered it.

"Hey, it's me," said the distinct voice of our two seat.

"Hi Porgy," I said. "What's up?" In the background I could hear a chaotic chorus of other voices shouting at one another.

"You guys definitely need to come and check out our suite," he said.

"Why?" I said. "What's so special about it?"

"Well, for starters, we have a minibar. And we've just invented a new game called Pillow Fight Jousting."

"What's that?"

"You'll just have to come and see for yourselves!" he said.

"OK, fine. But I hope you guys haven't been drinking . . ."

"No way! Not until after the race," Porgy assured me.

Peter and I grabbed our jackets and made our way over to join the bow four, after saying our goodbyes to Lisa. It was nearly time to head out for dinner. When we arrived at their suite, a loud commotion could be heard within, which became louder when Joe opened the door. Dak and Henry were already there, standing inside the room with their arms folded.

"You're just in time," Joe said. "Wean and Rob are about to engage in mortal combat!"

"Excellent," Peter said, smiling apologetically at a passing hotel guest, who gave us a brief look of disappoval.

The suite was in pretty bad shape. The blankets and sheets had been stripped from the beds and lay strewn about the floor, along with some dirty workout clothes. On the two double beds, Wean and Rob faced each other, pillows in hand, wearing nothing but their boxers.

"In this corner," Porgy announced through a rolled-up magazine, "Wearing the red shorts, we have the contestant from Portsmouth, Rhode Island—the indomitable Wean."

"YEAH!" Henry cheered.

Wean bounced around the bed like it was a trampoline, pumping his free hand in the air like a wild bronc rider.

"Next, from Longmeadow, Massachusetts, wearing the white and blue striped shorts—the raging bull, Rob Leavitt!"

"YEAH!!!" Joe cheered.

"Contestants, prepare yourselves for battle," Porgy announced.

Rob and Wean both started jumping up and down on the beds, as they prepared to lunge at each other in midair. The objective, Joe explained to us, was to make it to the other bed, while dealing a blow to your opponent. The space between the beds was considered a moat, and if you fell into it, you immediately lost the tournament.

"1, 2, 3 . . . GO!" Porgy shouted.

Wean and Rob lunged forward, flying through the air as they swung their pillows at one another. At the apex of their jump, both of them collided and fell down into the space between the beds.

"OW!" Rob called. "I think I sprained my ankle."

"Low blow," Wean said, complaining.

Just then Heidi walked in, dressed up and ready for dinner.

"What's going on here?" she said.

Joe briefly explained.

"All right, stop it, you idiots!" Heidi commanded. "Someone's going to get hurt!"

The tone of her voice had an immediate effect, for both Rob and Wean turned toward her in surprise.

"What's your problem?" Wean said, holding up his arms in protest.

"For God's sake, get dressed," Heidi said. "You both look ridiculous!"

Philadelphia may have had its urban charm and raw energy, but Peter's house in Wayne was part of the Main Line area that lay just outside the city limits, where big lawns and country clubs offered a slice of suburban tranquility. His spacious backyard had a brick patio and a well-manicured garden, which sloped down to a mill-pond filled with white geese. We all got drinks and spread out into the backyard, trying to behave ourselves. Peter's dad took up the role as grill master, plying us with burgers until we were stuffed, and his mother finished us off with a plate of cupcakes to fortify our emaciated bodies. The food, and the elegant surroundings, seemed to have a mollifying effect on everyone. Before we left, Charlie gathered us all inside to thank our hosts.

"Well, here's to a fantastic season," he said. "I have great expectations for you guys tomorrow, but whatever happens, I'm proud of you!" He raised a glass of club soda to the group, who fell silent in the shower of such affectionate praise.

"And just remember," Charlie added, "a day from now, you'll be drinking beer instead of soda!"

Everyone cheered.

"But not too much!" Peter's mother chimed in.

"Absolutely," Peter assured her.

There was still plenty of daylight as we shuttled back to the city, and crossing over the Girard Avenue Bridge we could see that many crews were still out on the river.

"Look," Rob said. "There's the statue of William Penn, and from this angle he looks like a wanker!"

Everyone glanced out the window to see the maligned historic statue.

"Crap! We forgot to run the steps at the Museum of Art," Joe suddenly remembered.

"We can do it tomorrow, after the race," Dak said.

"No way," Joe said. "That'll be too late. Besides, you know we're not going to sleep tonight anyway!"

"All right," Dak consented. "But let's make it quick. Everyone meet in the lobby in ten minutes."

Most of us still had our dinner clothes on as we made our way over to the northwest end of the Ben Franklin Parkway known as Eakins Oval, where the statue of George Washington riding on a horse stood. Just beyond it lay the Philadelphia Museum of Art. Even at the end of the day, it was an impressive sight, designed to resemble a Greek temple. The front portico, set back well beyond the broad entryway stairs, was held up by eight stone pillars and adorned with classical-looking bronze statuary.

"C'mon let's go!" Joe said.

We raced up the six flights of shallow steps that were laid out in sets of twelve, for a total of seventy-two. At the top of the fifth flight was a water fountain set in a big stone courtyard, and we jogged around it, making mock boxing gestures, as the pantheon of Greek gods and goddesses looked down at us from the rooftops.

"We are the champions!" Joe sang out.

"Not yet," Dak pointed out. "We still have to race, and win."

There was still an hour or so before sunset, and the sun was touching the trees and the river and turning everything to gold. There was a freshness to the May air as we walked through Fairmount Park and past Boathouse Row, finally reaching the grandstands that marked the finish line of the racecourse, where we all took turns climbing up and touching the green statue of Jack Kelly for good luck. Heidi silently conferred with Dak, pointing at the lane markers, while the rest of us stood gazing at the current and the random crews rowing past.

"Take a good long look," Joe whispered to me. "Then imagine yourself crossing that finish line in first place before you go to sleep tonight."

I nodded and smiled.

The old boathouses, and the huge flotilla of crews in Philadelphia, were an inspiration to anyone who rowed. We stood there for a moment and let it soak in. Then we slowly walked back to Boathouse Row and watched the last crews land and put their boats away. As the sun set, strings of white lights blinked on and outlined the rooflines and archways of the little boathouses, illuminating the eclectic group of buildings and making the entire east bank of the river look grand and festive. As we wandered back to our hotel, my crewmates and I drifted farther apart, strung out into different subgroups again. Everyone was engaged in their own thoughts and private conversations, but there was still enough light for me to notice that the cherry trees were just starting to blossom, and I had the notion that everything living was about to emerge, just waiting for the sun's blessing.

Chapter Twenty-Three

A Good Victory Lasts Forever

"TRINITY, LANE 1. COXSWAIN, PLEASE RAISE YOUR HAND. COAST GUARD, LANE 2. COXSWAIN, PLEASE RAISE YOUR HAND . . ."

As the starting line referee went down the line of freshman lightweight crews, checking in with each coxswain, all six teams sat ready and waiting, their sterns held fast to anchored stake boats. Every muscle in our bodies was wound to maximum recoil, and our ears were primed to listen for the starting commands. We knew the start would come quickly once the boats were aligned and all the coxswains' hands were down. Then we would sprint forward, with every ounce of energy our 149-pound bodies could muster.

"Two seat, take a stroke!" Heidi called out. Porgy responded, resetting our point.

"OARSMEN, SIT READY!" the starter commanded.

We slid back up to half-slide position, buried our blades, and sat up tall. Our blue and gold singlets were brilliant and distinct among the other crews, for they had been skillfully handmade by the mother of one of the guys on the varsity lightweight team, David Bolster. The Coast Guard coxswain raised his hand suddenly in order to make a last-second point adjustment. Georgetown did the same, and then all the crews were set and ready again.

The wind was minimal, and the skies slightly overcast—ideal conditions for a fast race.

"ALL HANDS ARE DOWN," the starter barked. "SIT READY . . . READY ALL, ROOOOW!"

We came off the line at a forty-two and then settled to a comfortable thirty-four. Our start was clean, with no crabs, and soon we were out ahead and moving well, locking into a sustainable rhythm.

"WE HAVE A LENGTH," Heidi called out.

When you rocket forward off the starting line of a six-boat race, part of you just holds on for dear life. Your mind immediately begins to enter a different state of reality, induced by the fight-or-flight response and the adrenaline-laced blood coursing through your veins. For me, an inner battle emerged, equal in intensity to the one visible around us. It was located in the dark recesses of my brain, and it was filled with the raw material that dreams are made of—both good and bad. I automatically started to have conversations in my head that supplanted anything that Heidi was saying. *You can do this . . . no you can't . . . shut up and just row . . . don't mess up!* Suddenly I didn't know a thing, other than the fact that I held an oar in my hands.

Soon I couldn't even remember what other boats were in our race, but it hardly mattered. It was simply Trinity versus Coast Guard. That morning both crews had gone through the semis in first and second place, beating all the times in the other heats. But we'd only edged the Guard by a half second, or about two seats. And now we had to do it all over again.

"POWER TEN!" Heidi called out, trying to break away into open water. "1, 2, 3, 4 . . ."

Our boat lifted off, and I heard the magic gurgle under our hull, telling us that we were moving well. Once you've beaten someone once, you know you can do it again, and the psychology is definitely in your favor. And while our victory against Coast Guard back in April may have been a fluke, it wasn't any longer. We'd taken them again that morning—not by much, but enough to establish a clear pattern of dominance.

"GIVE ME TEN AND SHOW ME YOU ARE MEN!" the Coast Guard coxswain demanded with unadulterated anger in his voice.

The Guard pushed back into us, restoring a bow-to-stern overlap. We were now approaching the Strawberry Mansion Bridge, where the course would shift right and the other crews would gain some ground on us. We'd planned a silent power twenty to try to compensate.

"HERE WE GO!" Heidi cued us with excitement in her voice.

Make no mistake, crew racing is a naval battle, and the maneuvering in a six-boat race can be highly strategic. As the clear favorite, however, our strategy was quite simple—get ahead and stay ahead. The longer we did so, the longer Coast Guard would suffer from the notion of being second best. We also knew it had to irk them that we had a woman in our boat, guiding our efforts.

"C'MON, WE'RE MOVING ON THEM!" the Coast Guard cox'n shouted.

Sports writers try to describe crew races in print, but it's generally a useless exercise. Sure, they can list stroke ratings, and how the lead changed back and forth between crews, but these are just the superficial details. What they generally fail to convey are the raw feelings that surround the immediacy of the moment. Then again, ask an oarsman to remember a race, and be prepared for gobbledygook.

"COAST GUARD JUST TOOK TWO SEATS ON US! LET'S TAKE IT UP TWO!" Heidi shouted.

Peter bumped it up to a thirty-eight. We were now one thousand meters from the finish line, barely holding onto a three-quarter-length lead.

An oarsman's mind during a race is, at best, empty of discernable content. Sure, you might experience individual feelings of rage, excitement, and fear, and I certainly had all of those bouncing around in my brain. But what saved you from being overpowered by these transient emotions was your training. It had to, or you were totally screwed—distracted by their siren's call.

"C'mon!" Peter shouted. "Pull harder!" He had a white piece of cloth tied around his mop of brown hair, making him look like a Samurai. As if in response, one of the guys in the Coast Guard boat let out a primal scream, and the sound went straight through my gut like an arrow.

Eight guys dealing with their own neurosis and ideas about how a race should be rowed was not a real crew, it was a catastrophe. By contrast, a well-trained crew was like a synchronized machine with eight cylinders. One stroke followed another in near-perfect succession, seemingly devoid of individual nuance. And so the main question now was, which crew could keep it together? Certainly there was an advantage to being ahead, but there were disadvantages too. As the top-seeded crew, the race was now ours to lose. Coast Guard was still sitting on our stern, like a hungry shark, keeping the pressure on. Only 750 meters remained, but my legs already felt spent, waterlogged with lactic acid. And with every stroke, the Guard was eating away at our lead.

Up until this point, the race had been a game of chess, played out between the two coxswains. Each time Coast Guard had moved on us, Heidi had called for a countermove. Each coxswain knew what his or her crew was capable of and just how hard he or she could push them. But now we were like two tired boxers in the final rounds of a match, each one hoping that the other would falter. To make matters worse, the other four crews in the race had sensed our fatigue and were now making a final charge of their own. In lane six Georgetown had actually gained overlap on Coast Guard.

"SPRINT!" Heidi yelled. "SPRINT!"

Fear either overcomes and paralyzes you, or you learn to ride it like a wave. I felt a second boost of adrenaline kick in, giving us a final push. Five boats were now closely overlapped, surging toward the line. As we flew past the stoic figure of Jack Kelly, we barely heard the cheers from the grandstands, now rising to a distant roar.

"DO IT FOR CHARLIE!" Heidi shouted.

As young oarsmen in an undefeated crew, we'd begun to think of ourselves as invincible superheroes, yet deep within we knew that it was mostly our coach who had made us what we were at that moment. Charlie Poole had been our Prometheus, the invisible "tenth member" of our crew, and he had given us our life force. So in that last twenty strokes it was our coach who helped carry us across the line.

An air horn blasted once, then twice, seconds apart, indicating the close margin between the first two boats. We immediately stopped and fell over our oars. I saw Peter pound his fists on the top of his legs, trying to take away the burning sensation.

When the six eights had drifted to a standstill, I looked over at Caluso, slumped over his oar. Wincing in pain and still gasping for breath, he finally glanced over at me, and when our eyes met, the official announcement came over the loudspeaker—we'd won by a margin of 1.5 seconds over Coast Guard. I couldn't help myself as I joined Peter and pumped my fist in the air and then released my own jubilant howl. Peter turned around and we hollered together.

Caluso shook his head and looked away in disbelief, utterly defeated. I suddenly felt badly for him, sensing his despair. Even though he'd been such a jerk to me in the past, any resentment I held toward him suddenly dissolved in that moment of victory. It felt incredibly good to win, of course, but my motivation for placing first no longer relied on disliking him. Much later it occurred to me that how you feel about your own performance is what really matters, and your opponent is only there to keep you honest and on your game.

There is a druglike bliss to winning, and it temporarily makes the world around you seem quite wonderful. At the awards dock, Charlie Poole was waiting for us, dressed in his red, white, and blue Bermuda shorts, track sweatshirt, and official Dad Vail cap. He gave us a toothy smile, and we could see the tears welling up in his eyes.

"I'm so proud of you guys," he said, his voice hoarse from cheering. "I can't tell you how much this means to me."

Soon he had to stop talking and resorted to giving everyone a giant-size Charlie Poole hug. None of us could speak, and as the cameras clicked, we stood there like a bunch of dopes, unpracticed in the ways of winning. Even Karma Joe, who was normally the most reserved of the lot, was beside himself with childish joy, and Wean kept hugging Heidi as if they were sweethearts.

Once the Dad Vail stewards had placed the medals around our necks, we got back in our boat and rowed back to Undine. Free to become spectators for the rest of the afternoon, we ran back to the course to watch the rest of our crews. In between races we ran up and down Kelly Drive, collecting our betting shirts, with our gold medals still slung around our necks. Most of the teams we beat were gracious, and openly offered us their congratulations. Then we circled back to Undine and helped the final Trinity crews land.

The women's varsity had just returned to the dock, wearing silver medals around their necks and looking happy. We collected their oars for them, and everyone clapped as they took their boat out of the water. Cynda Davis was grinning from ear to ear, momentarily at a loss for words, and my erstwhile date Kooshe looked totally ripped and confident—a total transformation from the shy girl I had met last fall. I felt an overwhelming sense of pride for them, even though they had narrowly lost to Ithaca College, taking second. Otherwise their season had been perfect.

Our freshman heavies had also done exceptionally well that day, considering they'd only managed one victory prior to the Dad Vails. Sam Bradshaw had stroked his crew to a tremendous effort in the final sprint of their race, moving them from fifth to second place within the last thirty strokes. A silver medal was a total surprise. The varsity lights and the novice women also both came away with a bronze.

Finally, while Mongo and the varsity heavies failed to medal in the finals, they had rowed their hearts out just to qualify during the semi, taking second in a photo finish. In the final, they ended up a respectable fifth, as did our varsity heavyweight four. When all of these results had been officially tallied, Norm Graf gathered us all together at Undine dock to make the big announcement. Trinity had taken the Jack Bratten Points Trophy for overall best performance, unseating the previous year's winner, Coast Guard, forty-eight to forty-four.

Hoots and hollers were heard all around.

"Coach," Carl Rox finally asked, "does this mean we can destroy some capillaries tonight and get weak in the knees?"

Graf grinned, and then put on one of his mock frowns of disapproval.

"First, you have to load the shell trailer and make it back to Hartford," he bellowed. "After that, I'm off duty."

CHAPTER TWENTY-FOUR

All Rivers Lead to the Sea

Athletic glory may be fleeting and ephemeral, but the memory of a good victory can last a long time.

The bus ride back to Trinity was uneventful, as post-race exuberance gave way to fatigue. Daylight fell, and the quiet hum of the diesel engine had a soporific effect. Soon everyone was draped over their gear or each other, hovering on the verge of sleep. Some unlikely pairings emerged in the darkness, including Cynda Davis with her head on Carl Rox's lap, and Heidi and Wean leaning shoulder to shoulder, signaling a potential budding romance. People had let their guard down a bit, now that racing season was over. As we neared Hartford, the familiar smell of unwashed athletes grew progressively more intolerable, and a brief pit stop for dinner at a McDonald's only made matters worse.

"For Chrissakes, this bus smells like a cattle car!" Norm Graf observed, causing those among us who were still awake to break out into a chorus of barnyard noises.

"Mooo . . ."

"Eye-Aw . . ."

"Baaaa . . ."

"Cockadoodle-doo!"

The intense physical demands of rowing had definitely brought out our base nature, and I was looking forward to rebalancing my daily life, now that the season had finally ended. Rowing had rendered a lot of rewards, including a nice gold medal, but it had also extracted a heavy toll. When you see oarsmen literally collapse after a hard race, or even black out, it tells you something important about the sport. In rowing, there is virtually no way to avoid the painful experience of going into oxygen deficit, which is a gut-wrenching endeavor. You are driven deeper into it by the fact that you don't want to let your teammates down, and they in turn help push you beyond your limits. But with each successive race, this intense form of cardiovascular distress becomes less appealing to all but those who enjoy pain. Beyond the physical component of discomfort, which is only temporary, also comes an expectation that creates a patterned response in the brain.

And this, for many, becomes difficult to give up.

We had become champions in our small sphere of endeavor, but now it was time to reenter normal society, and regain some sense of normalcy in our lives. As freshmen none of us knew what that would look or feel like, but for the moment, in the immediate aftermath of the Dad Vails, mostly we rested. The entire season, culminating with the National Championships, had required a Herculean commitment of time and energy. Now, at last, we could take a break. Yet even that would prove more challenging than it might appear.

Before I dozed off, I replayed our final race in my mind, and the moments afterward, when I'd collected all of the betting shirts that now lay beside me.

Surprisingly I was never able to find my own nemesis, Samuel Caluso, after the finals, even though I hung out for several minutes at the Coast Guard trailer. His teammate Gerald finally gave me a betting shirt and shook my hand in his stead.

Caluso had disappeared forever, like a bad dream.

— ❦ —

Back at Trinity most people didn't really take much notice of us, as rowing was not a big deal to the main student body. If you wanted athletic accolades, you played football. Still, we did receive some kudos in the days following the National Championships. Karma Joe got his picture splashed across the front cover of the *Trinity Reporter*, the college alumni magazine, and Norm Graf promised to let me take home a single scull to train, which would ironically prove to be the beginning of the end of my sweep rowing career.

Before that, however, the immediate benefit of finishing our last race was that we were now officially free of training rules. A celebratory night out was definitely in order, and the Trinity Pub fit the bill. As any elite athlete in training can attest, the first sip of beer after a long period of sobriety tastes like the nectar of the gods and produces a divine effect on both the palate and the brain. Both are surprised and delighted and then rendered numb to all of the cares of the world. The pitchers flowed all night long, until we were eventually kicked out to migrate over to the fraternities.

Henry Cropsey, who hoped to be rushed the following year at St. Anthony's, produced his bagpipes and began to march up and down Summit Avenue dressed in his kilt, playing "Amazing Grace" over and over again. When the campus police finally arrived and told him to pack it in, another member of the heavyweight team, who lacked any formal musical training, climbed up on top of the AD fraternity hall and proceeded to howl at the moon until the wee hours of the night.

In short, we did little to endear ourselves to the rest of the college.

Just after I made it safely back to my room and laid on my bed, fully clothed, there was a knock at my door. My roommate Jim answered.

"Hey Dan. It's some girl who says she knows you," he said, a bit surprised. Then, turning over his shoulder and half closing the door, he whispered: "She looks pretty cute—you'd better get your butt out of bed!"

It was Laurie Shields, the seven seat from the freshman women's team.

"I heard that you know how to climb the chapel," she said. "Want to show me how?" Her voice was a bit loud; she clearly had been celebrating.

"Uh—sure," I said, trying not to look too eager.

As we made our way out of the dorm, arm in arm, we suddenly came upon Dak and Porgy, who were just returning from the pub. Dak was wheeling his ten-speed bicycle and leaning on it heavily as he made his way forward.

"Can we help?" Porgy asked, smiling.

"Yes, may we be of assistance?" Dak offered, and then belched loudly, having drunk an impressive quantity of beer that night.

Laurie laughed. Everyone was in high spirits.

"No thanks, guys. I think we can manage this on our own," I said.

"Yes, Dak," Laurie agreed. "But we'll take that bike from you!"

She grabbed Dak's ten-speed and broke into a run before he had time to react.

"Stop! Thief!" he cried in jest.

"Remember all of my dating tips," Porgy shouted as I ran after her into the night.

Needless to say, we never made it to the chapel.

Epilogue

The next morning was less inspiring, as were the days that followed. Final papers and exams were due, and after that came a quick and unceremonious departure from the dorms. Once spring term ends at a small college like Trinity, a massive stampede ensues that rivals the running of the bulls in Pamplona. In the aftermath I felt curiously let down and at a loss of what to do with myself, particularly without the structure and rigor of rowing. Athletes thrive on their daily dose of endorphins, and without it they become restless and sometimes even despondent. The world around them becomes gray and dull. There is usually only one good solution, which is to start training again as soon as possible.

It's weird to go back home after being away at school freshman year, especially when you come from a small town. At first you are surrounded by the comfort of familiar things and people—parents, siblings, and old high school friends. All of these reinstate a sense of one's identity, but there is an oddness to the whole experience, for life has changed despite the sameness of things. My old room was waiting for me, looking just as it had when I left it, but now it felt more like a museum of sorts, filled with bits and pieces of my past life—a baseball glove that I no longer used, an old judo trophy gathering dust. My dog Schatz sniffed all of my new belongings as I unpacked, trying to assess what sort of life I'd led away from him. Then he cocked his head to one side as if to say, "Why didn't you take me with you?"

After a few days I was still feeling out of sorts, so my mother trucked me off to the local clinic to get a physical. My family doctor drew some blood, ran some tests, and confirmed that my white blood cell counts were still extremely low, as if they'd been through a massive battle. He speculated that I'd rowed through mononucleosis for the last part of the season and then lectured me on the dangers of overtraining. I told him that I didn't have a choice. I was lucky, he said, that I'd made it all the way through freshman crew season, then he cautioned me about liver damage. Rest was the prescription, and the Connecticut seashore provided the perfect solution for me to take my respite from rowing.

I found an outdoor job at the local Cedar Island Marina, helping yachts and pleasure cruisers find berths for the night or to simply gas up for a day's outing. It was good physical work, and it put me near the water. After a few weeks the sun and the salt air worked their simple magic, and soon I was nearly back to full health. But seeing the boats come and go all day at the marina made me long to be back in a shell again and moving over water. The rowing bug had not yet left my body.

So I began to venture out into Long Island Sound, in the big Pocock wherry that Norm Graf had lent me. With its high gunnels and wide beam, it was the perfect craft for the unpredictable conditions of open water. Most people in town had never seen a rowing shell before, and didn't know what to make of the twenty-foot-long rowing vessel. Power boaters were also ignorant of the tippy nature of my little boat, but with practice I found that I could actually surf on their passing wakes if I positioned myself perpendicular to them and accelerated my strokes at just the right time. When I caught a wave, the little wherry would suddenly lift off and then shoot forward with great speed, making my entire sea-rowing enterprise more adventurous and fun.

I rowed across the town harbor to Cedar Island and then up the nearby Hammonasset River. Sometimes I even brought lunch with me, or a fishing line to troll off the back of the boat for blues. During those leisurely summer rows, I often thought about the season that had just ended and took pleasure in reliving the very best moments in my mind. The action of rowing, where you face backward as you progress, has an effect on one's memory in this way. Water, too, is a natural medium for self-reflection. Mostly, though, I reveled in the new strength that had grown inside of me during the year, which now flowed through my hands as I held two oars. After a particularly long row, after I'd returned home and was sitting quietly at the dinner table, my father would sometimes ask me, "What is it about rowing that is so appealing?" I would just shrug, unable to articulate the sense of calmness that came upon me, post-row.

In the smallest scheme of things, rowing had given me a sense of personal accomplishment, and I felt like I could do almost anything now. After all, I'd worked hard and become a part of a championship crew and overcome a bully who had plagued me during high school. But beyond this lay something much larger, and I could feel this, too, as I rowed, like a second heartbeat. It was the sense of being part of a crew. With my teammates I'd accomplished more than I could have ever imagined and done things I never would have done alone. So much of my time in high school had been spent on setting myself apart and rising above the pack, but in crew I had learned a much different lesson—the unique sense of being that emerges when one's movements are given over to others. It was a paradox that might have taken me years to unravel without the direct experience of rowing that year, guided by such an excellent, caring coach.

A single scull, which I could pilot alone, lent me an immediate sense of freedom again, but it would never replicate the thrill of crew racing in eights, and I knew it. Still, as I took those solo journeys out to sea, I knew that I'd never lose the memory of my teammates inspiring me forward with every stroke I took.

Acknowledgments

I'd like to thank Ed Hewitt, founder of row2k.com, for editing and publishing the preliminary chapters of this book online; my wife Karen Barss, for doing the bulk of the editing; Goran Buckhorn, whose excellent rowing blog, "Hear the Boat Sing" added historical context and additional graphics; Christina Bleyer, director of Special Collections and Archives at the Watkinson Library, Trinity College, for photo permissions, as well as Rand Pearsall and the *Trinity Reporter*, for the use of photographs of Trinity Crew. Also a big thanks to all of the guys on my team that year, my freshman coach Charlie Poole, and head coach Norm Graf, who recently passed away at age ninety-three after spending fifty years in the sport of rowing.

Index